Ecosystem Economics for Modern Associations

How Participation, Governance, and Platform Thinking Reshape Value Creation

Sean M Johnson

Lakefield Drive Publishing
Townsville, Queensland

lakefield
drive

Published 2025
by Lakefield Drive Publishing,
Lakefield Drive Pty Ltd
Townsville, Queensland, Australia

National Library of Australia Cataloguing-in-Publication Data
Johnson, Sean M. author.
Ecosystem Economics for Modern Associations: How Participation, Governance, and Platform Thinking Reshape Value Creation

Townsville, Queensland: Lakefield Drive Publishing, 2025.
Includes bibliographical references.

Identifiers:
ISBN: 978-1-7640727-4-8 (ebook (pdf))
ISBN: 978-1-7640727-5-5 (Paperback)
ISBN: 978-1-7640727-6-2 (Kindle (EPUB))

Subjects:
LCSH: Associations, Management. | Business models, Nonprofits. | Governance, Associations and clubs. | Strategic planning, Membership organisations.

Classification:
LCC HD2741 | DDC 658.048, dc23
LC record available at N/A

Typeset in Georgia and Aptos by Lakefield Drive Publishing

For more information, visit: lakefielddrive.co

Connect with the Author: sean@lakefielddrive.co

In Memory of Barry

Preface

Ecosystem Economics for Modern Associations: How Participation, Governance, and Platform Thinking Reshape Value Creation is the companion book to *The Modern Association Playbook. The latter* was written to catalyse action. It offered a practical, step-by-step guide for association leaders to rethink strategy, modernise governance, and build platforms capable of sustaining relevance and trust in a fast-changing world. But beneath every strategic shift lies an economic logic. This companion book exists to unpack that logic, and to equip leaders, analysts, and policy thinkers with the tools to interrogate, design, and future-proof the value systems that underpin modern associations.

Associations today operate as economic actors, but they do so outside traditional market norms. They coordinate participation, broker trust, and facilitate value in ecosystems where profit is not the sole objective. This complexity requires its own economic architecture, one that blends platform theory, incentive design, governance dynamics, and public value framing into a coherent analytical foundation.

This book is not a rehash of the Playbook. It is the scaffolding behind it. A guide not just for what to do, but why it works, and when it doesn't.

Sean M Johnson

Disclosure

This book reflects the synthesis of extensive professional experience, original intellectual frameworks, and a commitment to supporting associations as they navigate change. The author acknowledges the support of a range of digital research and writing tools that assisted in shaping, editing, and refining the manuscript. These include artificial intelligence tools such as ChatGPT (OpenAI), and Perplexity based AI models, which were used under human supervision to support research collation, enhance clarity, and streamline editing processes and generate pictures.

All ideas, analysis, and frameworks presented in this book remain the intellectual property of the author drawing on a wider range of literature. No generative tool was used to substitute for professional judgement, theoretical development, or the original articulation of concepts central to this work. Care has been taken to critically assess, adapt, and validate any content derived from digital assistance to ensure it reflects the strategic, legal, and governance standards expected of a professional publication.

Where third-party material or references have been used, they have been cited in the Bibliography. All case studies are either based on publicly available information, used with permission, or anonymised and adapted for illustrative purposes.

This book was independently published by Lakefield Drive Pty Ltd, with editorial direction and publication design overseen by the author.

Note on Sources

This playbook synthesises concepts from a wide range of governance, economic, and platform design literature. While the text is original, it draws conceptually on the work of authors such as Elinor Ostrom, Oliver Williamson, Ronald Coase, Jean Tirole, ISO 37000 governance standards, and others. A complete reference list is provided at the end of the book. Specific diagnostic tools and strategic models have been developed by the author unless otherwise stated.

About the Author

Sean M Johnson is a governance advisor, company secretary, researcher, and strategy consultant with a career spanning law, policy, education, and digital transformation. He has worked with national associations, not-for-profit boards, professional bodies, regulators and industry peak organisations to rethink governance, develop future-focused strategy, and implement change with impact.

A Fellow of the Governance Institute of Australia, Sean combines practical boardroom experience with deep expertise in risk, regulation, and strategic innovation. His approach is grounded in systems thinking and informed by both economic theory and real-world practice.

Across his work with association leaders, Sean has seen a consistent pattern: legacy systems, good intentions, and hard work are no longer enough. Navigating today's complexity requires new frameworks, ones that integrate platform thinking, governance agility, and digital enablement.

This book brings together Sean's experience in advising, designing, and leading association transformations. It is shaped by years of collaboration with CEOs, boards, and change agents committed to building organisations that are not only sustainable, but future-ready.

Table of Contents

Part I: The Story is in the Numbers

Understanding the Economic Shifts Reshaping Associations

To lead in a platform-enabled world, associations must do more than update programs or adopt new technology, they must rewire how they think about value, participation, and purpose. That rewiring begins with economics.

This section lays the analytical foundations for the journey ahead. It explores the structural shifts redefining the associative form, not just as a governance entity, but as an economic actor embedded in networks of trust, contribution, and exchange. From the collapse of information scarcity to the rise of multisided value creation, these changes aren't just external pressures, they are signals of a deeper systemic realignment.

The numbers tell the story: declining retention, stagnant revenue per member, fragmented engagement. But behind the metrics lie dynamics, platform logics, incentive architectures, and economic feedback loops, that must be understood if they are to be designed for.

In Part I, we reframe associations as platforms of coordinated participation. We introduce the core economic principles that underpin this model, and we begin to answer the critical question:

If associations are no longer just service providers, what, exactly, are they becoming?

Chapter 1. Why Economic Thinking Matters

Setting the Stage: More Than Mission

Associations are not just mission-driven organisations, they are economic actors. Whether they realise it or not, every decision they make about structure, membership, pricing, and participation rests on implicit economic assumptions. These assumptions shape how value is created, who contributes to it, how revenue is earned, and how costs, both financial and social, are managed.

As the association sector navigates a period of profound disruption, the need to make these assumptions explicit has never been more urgent. Member expectations have shifted from passive receipt to active participation. Revenue streams once taken for granted, dues, events, and sponsorships, are fragmenting. Technology platforms now mediate engagement, not just deliver services. And governance systems are under strain, stretched between oversight, agility, and trust.

Economic thinking helps leaders make sense of this. Not to turn associations into businesses, but to understand how they function as systems of value exchange, and how they must evolve to remain viable, legitimate, and impactful.

From Service Provider to Platform Orchestrator

In *The Modern Association Playbook*, we introduced the idea of the association as a *platform,* a facilitator of interaction, co-creation, and shared outcomes. That model challenged the assumptions of Association 1.0: centralised delivery, static value, and one-directional engagement.

But behind that structural shift is an economic one. Platform associations operate according to a different logic, where value emerges not from what the association produces, but from what it enables others to create.

Understanding this shift means engaging with foundational economic principles: network effects, transaction costs, externalities, and scaling dynamics. These aren't abstract ideas, they are the mechanisms through which associations generate value, risk, and relevance. These are attributes that many associations are neglecting and failing to capture the latent vale.

Why Traditional Models Are Under Strain

Most legacy associations were built on a *cost-recovery model.* Services were priced to cover expenses, not to scale impact. Value was measured in outputs delivered, not outcomes achieved. This made sense when:

- Professional knowledge was scarce and centralised.

- Membership conferred exclusive access.
- Governance systems operated in a stable regulatory environment.

That world is gone. Today, associations compete not just with each other, but with platforms like LinkedIn, Slack, and Coursera. These platforms enable professionals to build networks, learn, and contribute, often for free, and often with more immediate feedback and reach.

Associations that continue to price for access rather than value, or operate as closed systems rather than open platforms, will struggle to remain relevant, or solvent.

What This Chapter Does

This chapter introduces the key economic concepts that underpin the platform model of associations. It sets the stage for the deeper analysis that follows by explaining:

Why linear cost-recovery models are fragile in a platform economy.

- How **network effects** shift the logic of value creation.
- How **transaction costs** are restructured by digital infrastructure.
- Why **externalities** must be governed, not ignored.
- What it means to evaluate association performance through an **economic lens**.

It then connects these concepts to practical realities: monetisation decisions, member participation design, risk and governance trade-offs, and strategic metrics.

In short: this chapter explains why economic thinking is not just relevant, but essential, and how it can equip leaders to design better associations for a complex, participatory, and impact-driven future.

Scene: The Cost of Doing Everything Right

The meeting started like so many others.

The Finance and Strategy Subcommittee had gathered for its quarterly review. The papers pre-read, the dashboards updated, nothing obviously off-track. Membership dues income was holding steady. Event registrations were down slightly, but within tolerance. A new sponsor had just signed on.

"*So why does it feel,*" the Treasurer finally asked, "*like we're working harder than ever... for less?*"

Silence.

The CEO, a former policy leader now juggling technology procurement, risk briefings, and member churn data, nodded slowly.

"*We're doing more than ever, more webinars, more micro-credentials, more stakeholder engagement. But the margins are getting tighter. Engagement is scattered. We're subsidising participation that doesn't always translate to retention or revenue.*"

The Head of Member Strategy added quietly, "*It's like we're delivering services... but not generating value.*"

That was the moment it landed.

Not just a budget challenge, or a staffing stretch, but an underlying economic mismatch. The association was operating with the structure of a service provider, but in a world that rewarded platforms.

The problem wasn't effort. It was logic.

Framing the Shift

This is the scene playing out across association boardrooms everywhere. Organisations are delivering more programs, more access, more personalisation, but seeing diminishing returns.

Why? Because the assumptions that underpin their business models haven't evolved. Behind every strategy, every engagement tactic, every pricing model is a set of economic beliefs, often unexamined, frequently outdated.

This chapter is about making those beliefs visible.

A Hidden Discipline

Economic thinking in associations is rarely taught, and even more rarely discussed. Yet every major decision, how to price access, design participation, measure value, or manage growth, is an economic one.

Until now, many associations have relied on inherited structures: fixed fees, bundled benefits, access-based monetisation. These made sense in a world of information scarcity and professional gatekeeping. But today's members inhabit a different world:

- Knowledge is abundant.
- Networks are distributed.
- Value is co-created, not delivered.
- Participation is fluid and episodic.

And platforms, not programs, are winning.

Why This Chapter Matters

Before we can redesign associations as adaptive, platform-enabled institutions, we need to rethink their economic architecture. This chapter lays the groundwork by:

- Introducing key economic principles relevant to association platforms.
- Explaining how value creation, exchange, and capture differ in networked models.
- Highlighting why transaction costs, network effects, and externalities must become board-level considerations.
- Framing economic design as a matter of governance, trust, and strategic foresight.

Because when associations don't understand their own economics, they end up doing everything right and still falling behind.

From Linear to Platform Value Models

Rewriting the Logic of Engagement and Exchange

After that boardroom realisation that more effort wasn't equalling more value the team did what associations often do: they commissioned a benchmarking review.

The results were confronting.

Their offerings were extensive. Their member benefits list read like a catalogue: CPD, journals, advocacy briefings, online forums, exclusive tools. Yet uptake was uneven. Retention was softening. New joiners were price-sensitive, disengaged, or simply indifferent. There was no clear line between what the association offered... and what members actually valued.

The consultants were blunt: "*You're still operating like a utility. But your members are living in a network.*"

This wasn't a performance issue. It was a value architecture issue.

The Linear Model: Service In, Payment Out

For decades, associations operated on a linear economic model, borrowed from industrial-era businesses. The logic was straightforward:

- The association produced value (services, content, certifications).
- Members consumed that value in exchange for a fee.
- Engagement was periodic, mostly transactional.

This model worked when:

- Access to knowledge was scarce.
- Professional gatekeeping conferred exclusivity.
- Associations were the primary infrastructure for connection and identity.

But that world no longer exists.

Today's professionals can build communities, access CPD, and participate in sector dialogue without ever joining a formal body. Engagement happens continuously, across channels, and on platforms designed for interaction.

The Platform Model: Value as Interaction

Platform models invert the old logic. Instead of producing value and handing it to members, the association becomes an orchestrator of interaction:

- Members, partners, and stakeholders co-create value.
- The association curates, enables, and governs the conditions of exchange.
- Growth isn't driven by more content, it's driven by more meaningful connections.

Table 1-1 Linear -v- Platform

Linear (Association 1.0)	Platform (Association 2.0)
Organisation as producer	Organisation as enabler
Value delivered through services	Value co-created through interactions
Revenue from access and transactions	Revenue from participation, data, and network effects
Growth through service expansion	Growth through user engagement and trust infrastructure

The Tension Associations Must Face

Here's the crux: many associations are still using linear pricing and governance structures to run what is now a networked, relational system. That's why so many feel misaligned, they're trying to monetise access while their members are seeking interaction. They're tracking outputs while their value is increasingly intangible.

Without recognising this shift, associations risk doubling down on the wrong levers. They are increasing services, lowering fees, launching one more campaign, all the while missing the deeper transformation required.

This chapter now turns to the economic concepts that explain why the shift to platform thinking is not just strategic, but structural. It will introduce network effects, transaction costs, and externalities, not as abstract theories, but as practical tools for leaders redesigning association value.

What Is a Multi-Sided Platform?

What is the Engine Behind Modern Value Exchange

Back in the strategy retreat, the association's CTO had shared an observation that landed awkwardly in the room.

"*If we were a tech company,*" she said, "*we'd be classified as a two-sided platform. But we're not acting like one.*"

A few directors nodded, unsure whether it was a compliment or a diagnosis.

She explained:

"*A multi-sided platform isn't just a place where services are delivered. It's an infrastructure that connects different types of users who benefit from interacting with each other. We have members, partners, learners, employers, sponsors, but we treat them as audiences, not participants in an ecosystem.*"

That moment reframed the problem.

The Basics: More Than Just a Marketplace

A multi-sided platform (MSP) is an economic and organisational model that enables value-creating interactions between two or more distinct groups of users, each of whom relies on the platform to connect with the others.

Think of platforms like:

- Uber: connects drivers and riders.
- LinkedIn: connects professionals, recruiters, advertisers, and educators.
- Airbnb: connects hosts and guests, with data and trust systems in between.

The platform's job is to facilitate interactions, not to deliver the product itself, but to design the conditions under which users can generate value for each other.

The result? The platform becomes more valuable as more users join and engage, because each side benefits from the participation of the others.

Uber Explained

To understand this, consider **Uber**:

- On one side are **riders** seeking affordable, convenient transport.
- On the other are **drivers** looking to earn income by offering rides.

Uber provides the *infrastructure*, including the app, pricing algorithms, trust systems (ratings, identity verification), payment processing, and data analytics, that allows both groups to interact efficiently.

Importantly, Uber does not own cars or employ drivers directly. Its value lies in *orchestrating the interaction*: minimising friction, increasing match quality, and aligning incentives. The more drivers on the platform, the more valuable it becomes to riders (shorter wait times, competitive pricing). The more riders join, the more attractive it becomes for drivers (higher utilisation, more income). This feedback loop is called a cross-side network effect.

Platform in Practice: A Shopping Centre as Multi-Sided Market

To further illustrate the concept of a multi-sided platform, consider the economics of a shopping centre.

At first glance, a shopping centre appears to be a real estate business, leasing space to retailers. But in reality, it functions as a classic multi-sided platform. It connects and creates value between several distinct user groups:

- **Retailers**, who seek access to high foot traffic, shared infrastructure, and visibility
- **Shoppers**, who value convenience, variety, and the curated experience of multiple brands in one place
- **Brands and advertisers**, who benefit from in-mall promotions, signage, and activations
- **Event partners**, who use the centre to reach targeted audiences
- **Property owners and investors**, who seek long-term yield and asset appreciation

The shopping centre's role is not to sell goods, but to design the conditions that allow these user groups to interact in mutually beneficial ways. It manages spatial layout, signage rules, common area maintenance, seasonal events, and traffic flows, all in service of amplifying the value created through those interactions.

The more high-quality stores that join, the more attractive the centre becomes to shoppers. The more shoppers it attracts, the more valuable the centre is to retailers. This is the dynamic of cross-side network effects. Importantly, the centre's success depends on its ability to balance the needs of all sides and continually adapt its design to maximise mutual benefit.

Associations can learn from this logic. Like shopping centres, they already host multiple user groups: members, employers, educators, sponsors, policymakers. Yet many still operate with a one-directional mindset, producing services and delivering them to members, rather than enabling value to emerge from interaction between participants.

By adopting a platform lens, associations can begin to reframe their role. The question becomes not "What should we provide?" but "What kinds of valuable interactions can we design, enable, and govern across our ecosystem?"

Why This Matters for Associations

Most modern associations already function like latent platforms, even if they haven't realised it:

- They connect members with each other (peer-to-peer).
- They connect members with employers (jobs boards, credentialing).
- They connect learners with content creators (CPD, webinars, mentoring).
- They connect sponsors with sector audiences (partnership programs).

But these interactions are often fragmented, under-designed, or unintentionally siloed. They lack the architecture, what is referred to as the governance, that gives true platforms their power: trust infrastructure, dynamic pricing, feedback loops, and value-sharing mechanisms.

To fully embrace platform economics, associations must stop asking, "*What can we offer our members?*" and start asking, "*What types of interactions are we enabling, and how do those interactions create mutual value?*"

Key Features of Multi-Sided Platforms

Table 1-2 Key Features of Multi-Sided Platforms

Feature	Implication for Associations
Multiple user groups	Members, employers, educators, partners, sponsors
Indirect value creation	One user group benefits from another (e.g. employers gain from certified members)
Network effects	More users = more value for all, if interaction is enabled
Intermediation logic	The association's role is to orchestrate, not own, all value exchange
Trust and governance infrastructure	Data, reputation, moderation, and transparency are core assets

The Realisation That Changes the Conversation

Once association leaders understand their organisation as a multi-sided platform, everything shifts:

- Membership strategy becomes ecosystem design.
- Revenue planning becomes monetisation architecture.
- Engagement metrics become interaction analytics.
- Governance becomes stewardship of a complex network.

This isn't a radical reinvention. It's a recognition of what associations already are, but this provides and a blueprint for what they can become.

Now that we've mapped the basic anatomy of a multi-sided platform, we can explore the economic engines that make them work, starting with the concept at the heart of all successful platforms: *network effects*.

Platform in Practice: A Member Association as a Multi-Sided Market

Let's now apply the concept of a multi-sided platform directly to the association sector.

Consider a national professional body representing allied health practitioners. On the surface, it might appear to be a traditional membership organisation, providing CPD, policy advocacy, and networking events in exchange for annual dues. But underneath, it already functions as a multi-sided platform with the potential to scale its impact.

It connects multiple distinct groups:

- Members, who seek learning, credentials, and career support
- Employers, who seek access to qualified professionals
- Education providers, who offer training aligned to industry standards
- Partners and sponsors, who seek trusted access to a targeted audience
- Government and regulators, who need input from a representative professional voice

- Patients and the public, who benefit indirectly from a strong, ethical profession

Each group derives value not only from the association directly, but from interacting with the other groups through the association's infrastructure. Members benefit from job boards and mentoring programs. Employers benefit from credential verification and advertising opportunities. Educators benefit from alignment with competency frameworks and access to learners. Sponsors gain visibility and engagement.

The association's role, like that of a shopping centre or digital platform, is to orchestrate these interactions, ensuring trust, alignment, and mutual benefit. This means designing systems for credentialing, recognition, matchmaking, feedback, and low-friction participation.

As more users engage, the network becomes more valuable for everyone, a hallmark of cross-side network effects. But only if the association sees itself not as a service provider, but as an interaction enabler.

When viewed through this lens, the questions facing association leaders shift:

- Not "*How do we deliver more member benefits?*"
- But "*How do we design high-value interactions between members, employers, educators, and others?*"
- Not "*How do we retain members?*"
- But "*How do we build trust infrastructure and co-created value that makes participation compelling?*"

This is the economic shift from Association 1.0 to Association 2.0 — from delivering content to enabling a connected ecosystem of value exchange.

Platform in Practice: A University as a Multi-Sided Market

Universities are often thought of as institutions that deliver education to students. But viewed through an economic lens, a university is a highly complex multi-sided platform connecting multiple stakeholder groups who each interact with and derive value from one another:

- Students, who seek credentials, learning experiences, and employment outcomes
- Academics, who seek research funding, publication opportunities, and teaching impact
- Employers, who seek work-ready graduates and applied research partnerships
- Government, which seeks policy advice, skilled workforce development, and regulated accreditation
- Alumni, who seek identity, lifelong learning, and professional networks
- Industry partners, who seek innovation, commercialisation, and talent pipelines

Each of these user groups depends not just on what the university provides, but on what the other groups contribute and how they interact. Employers value students more when they graduate with relevant skills. Students value institutions more when employers actively recruit from them. Researchers gain impact when their work reaches industry. Governments gain legitimacy through the knowledge outputs and equity reach of the sector.

Crucially, the university itself is not the sole producer of value. Instead, its platform role is to orchestrate connections, lower transaction costs (e.g. for industry–research engagement), and provide trust infrastructure (e.g. quality assurance, credentialing systems, and research integrity frameworks). The value is co-created.

This means designing:

- *Student–employer* engagement platforms (e.g. internships, career fairs)
- *Research translation* pathways (e.g. innovation precincts, licensing offices)
- *Alumni–student* mentoring programs
- *Industry–curriculum* feedback loops
- *Cross-sector data ecosystems* for impact measurement

Like any platform, the university becomes more valuable as participation across each group grows, provided it enables meaningful interaction and governs it well. These cross-side network effects are the engine of modern university value.

The implication is clear: the economics of higher education are no longer linear. Universities are not just content providers or service deliverers, they are platforms of participation, where value is increasingly relational, distributed, and co-produced.

Side Bar: Von Hippel Innovation and Member-Created Value

Associations operating as platforms increasingly benefit from what Jason Potts[1] term's "von Hippel innovation", a paradigm of innovation driven not by producers or firms, but by end users, members, and communities engaged in innovation and solving problems relevant to their own practice, often motivated by localised benefit, peer reputation, or learning rather than commercial returns.

In contrast to the traditional Schumpeterian model, where firms develop and monetise innovations, von Hippel innovation is decentralised, community-led, and fuelled by the sticky local knowledge of practitioners. Potts argues that such innovation is not only more democratised, but increasingly more effective as digital platforms reduce the cost of sharing, collaboration, and visibility.

For associations, this paradigm is profound. It implies that the most valuable innovations and content may emerge not from central programs, but from the members themselves, through peer-contributed knowledge hubs, member-led CPD, community toolkits, or even collaborative advocacy campaigns. A well-designed membership model should enable, recognise, and amplify this kind of user-led innovation.

In this way, membership becomes a mechanism not just for access, but for contribution, a platform through which members create value for others in the ecosystem. Supporting

---

[1] Potts, J. (2025). von Hippel innovation. Prometheus, 40(2), 74-91. Based on the insight of Eric von Hippel. See: Von Hippel, E. (2006). *Democratizing innovation*. the MIT Press.

this requires low-friction contribution pathways, recognition systems, and governance models that balance decentralised participation with trust and quality assurance.

Von Hippel innovation is produced faster, with lower cost, and better fit to real-world problems, because it is created by the people who need it. Associations that provide the platform infrastructure for this kind of innovation can dramatically expand their relevance and impact.

Chapter 2. Network Effects

Why more participants creates more value

Back in the retreat room, the consultant brought up a case study that turned a few heads.

"*Ever heard of Stack Overflow?*" he asked. "*They don't pay contributors. They don't produce the content. But they've built one of the most valuable knowledge ecosystems in tech.*"

The comparison felt jarring, what did a software Q&A site have to do with a membership association?

Everything, it turns out.

"*What makes Stack Overflow powerful,*" he continued, "*isn't what it knows, it's how it enables users to share what they know. The value grows as more people participate. That's a network effect. And associations are sitting on untapped network effects every day.*"

Defining Network Effects

A network effect occurs when the value of a product, service, or platform increases as more people use it.

There are two main types:

- **Direct network effects**: Every new user adds value to others of the same type. *Example*: The more members join a mentoring forum, the richer the pool of perspectives and experiences for everyone else.
- **Indirect network effects**: The addition of one group of users increases value for another group. *Example*: More credentialed members attract more employers; more employers create more value for members.

In multi-sided platforms, indirect network effects are the norm, and the engine.

Why Associations Struggle to Harness Them

Traditional association models often ignore or underutilise network effects. Instead of facilitating interaction, they focus on:

- Delivering content to passive recipients
- Selling access to pre-packaged services
- Managing member engagement as a consumption metric

This logic creates what economists call diminishing marginal returns, the more you produce, the more it costs, and the harder it is to scale.

By contrast, network effects create increasing returns: each new interaction adds cumulative value to the system. But only if:

- Users can find and interact with each other
- The association enables low-friction exchange
- There is a feedback loop that rewards participation

Network Effects in Action: A Credentialing Scenario

From CPD Provider to Ecosystem Orchestrator

Imagine a mid-sized association managing an online credentialing program.

Phase 1: Linear model: The association offers CPD courses and issues certificates. Members complete the courses, pay a fee, and receive formal recognition. The value is tied to how much content the association can produce or procure.

Phase 2: Indirect network effect: The association invites *employers* to verify credentials, leave endorsements, and post jobs. Now, each additional employer enhances the value of certification, not through the content, but through the recognition and career opportunities it unlocks.

Phase 3: Direct network effect: Certified members begin to review courses, mentor new learners, and share practical applications. The community becomes more active, self-reinforcing, and useful. The more they contribute, the more valuable the platform becomes for others.

The result? The association evolves from service deliverer to ecosystem orchestrator, with value growing from the interactions it enables, not just the content it controls.

Designing for Network Effects

To unlock network effects, associations must shift from content delivery to interaction enablement.

Table 2-1 Unlock network effects

Design Lever	Strategic Shift
Community architecture	From passive access → to collaborative, member-led networks
Credentialing systems	From static courses → to employer-integrated, verified pathways
Events and engagement	From broadcast sessions → to peer-driven, interactive formats
Technology stack	From siloed tools → to open, feedback-rich, participatory systems
Contribution pathways	From top-down programs → to crowdsourced knowledge and innovation

This is not about building "more tech." It's about creating the relational conditions in which members can create value for and with each other.

The Boardroom Insight

The Chair of the Finance and Strategy Subcommittee summed it up later:

"We've been trying to scale services. But what we should be doing is scaling interactions."

That's the economic power of network effects. When combined with smart governance and aligned incentives, they become one of the most powerful tools an association can harness, not just to grow, but to remain relevant.

Case 1: Peer-Led Mentoring Network

An association launches a mentoring platform. Initially, uptake is slow. But once early adopters begin sharing feedback and success stories, demand grows. More mentors join to give back, more mentees sign up due to positive word of mouth, and the platform's perceived value accelerates, without the association adding any new features. That is a direct network effect.

Case 2: Employer Engagement with Micro-Credentials

A health sector association offers micro-credentials to rural practitioners. It then partners with rural hospitals to guarantee interviews for credential-holders. As employers engage, member uptake of credentials spikes. That's an indirect network effect, one user group enhancing value for another.

Case 3: Event Platform with Peer Review

An annual conference opens a space for members to pitch and vote on breakout topics. Participation triples. More votes lead to better sessions, more engagement, and a wider range of member-led content. Now the event isn't just about attendance, it's about interaction. Network effects emerge when participants shape the experience.

Chapter 3. Transaction Costs

Why Coordination Gets Expensive, and What to Do About It

The next morning, the CEO sat down with her COO and Head of Digital to unpack the previous day's strategy session. There was still a lingering sense of discomfort, not about purpose or performance, but about friction.

"*We spend more time aligning teams than serving members,*" the COO said. "*Project scoping meetings, sponsor briefings, governance subcommittees, compliance reporting. Every new idea adds layers.*"

The CEO nodded. "*And no one's doing anything wrong. But somehow... it still feels slow.*"

That's when the digital lead spoke up:

"*What we're seeing isn't inefficiency. It's transaction cost drag.*"

What Are Transaction Costs?

In economic terms, transaction costs are the costs of coordinating action in a system. First framed by Ronald Coase and later expanded by Oliver Williamson, these costs include:

- Search and information costs, finding the right person, product, or data.
- Bargaining and decision costs, negotiating who does what, under what terms.
- Enforcement and compliance costs, ensuring rules are followed and disputes are resolved.

In market systems, transaction costs determine whether something is done internally or outsourced. In associations, they shape how easily people can work, share, decide, and engage.

Associations as Transaction Cost Managers

Historically, associations *existed* to reduce transaction costs:

- Members didn't need to individually source credible information, the association did it for them.
- Employers didn't need to vet qualifications manually, the association credentialed them.
- Stakeholders didn't need to coordinate policy input across a fragmented sector, the association convened it.

By creating standardisation, shared infrastructure, and common identity, associations made economic coordination easier. This is part of their often-overlooked public value.

But as digital tools have proliferated, and participation has become more distributed, the old methods of managing these costs, such as hierarchical governance, centralised services, bundled membership are now creating new forms of friction.

The Modern Frictions

Transaction costs haven't disappeared they've shifted. And in many associations, they've re-emerged in disguised forms:

Table 3-1 Transaction Costs

Type of Cost	How It Shows Up in Associations
Search Costs	Members can't find relevant CPD, employers struggle to reach talent
Decision Costs	Committees debate without authority clarity, pilots stall at sign-off
Enforcement Costs	Governance policies are hard to monitor or inconsistently applied
Trust Costs	Low transparency = stakeholder disengagement or sponsor pullback

These frictions don't just slow things down as they accumulate silently, draining value from even the best strategies. Like sand in an engine, they don't break it immediately but they wear it down. Think about frustrated members as they look to what they should be taking for CPD.

Transaction Costs as Governance Strain

Poorly managed transaction costs don't just show up in workflows, they show up in governance. When decision rights are unclear or reporting systems are rigid, boards spend more time *arbitrating exceptions* than stewarding strategy.

Symptoms of governance strain include:

- Strategic decisions delayed due to operational uncertainty
- Board committees consumed by tactical issues
- Disconnection between insight, authority, and action

This isn't about individual competence. It's a **design problem.** High transaction costs signal a mismatch between the association's governance infrastructure and the complexity of the system it seeks to coordinate.

Diagnostic: Transaction Cost Audit

Use this simple audit tool to assess where friction may be eroding your platform's performance:

Table 3-2 Transaction Cost Audit

Area	Prompt	Friction Rating
Search	Can members easily find relevant CPD, tools, or collaborators?	1 = high 5 = low
Decision	Are roles and decision rights clearly defined and delegated?	1 = high 5 = low)
Enforcement	Are policies consistently applied with minimal rework?	1 = high 5 = low)
Trust	Do stakeholders perceive transparency and fairness in engagement?	1 = high 5 = low)

Interpretation
Scores below 3 suggest areas where redesign or delegation may unlock significant coordination gains.

Designing to Reduce Transaction Costs

In a platform association, the goal is not to eliminate transaction costs, but to redesign how they are managed.

Table 3-3 Reducing Transaction Costs

Old Model	Platform-Enabled Design
Centralised staff as knowledge brokers	Member-to-member filtering, curated recommendations
Manual sponsorship negotiation	Tiered, self-service partner platforms
Top-down governance	Delegated decision rights, sandbox pilots, agile charters
Enforcement through rules	Moderation through social contracts, feedback systems

Transaction costs don't disappear in digital models, they shift. The question is whether your governance and infrastructure make it easier or harder for your network to coordinate, contribute, and trust.

Design Trade-Offs: Cost Reduction with Context

Every design decision introduces trade-offs. Reducing one type of transaction cost may increase another. The key is to be *intentional.*

Table 3-4 Design Trade-Offs in Transaction Cost Reduction

Lever	Benefit	Trade-Off
Delegated decision rights	Faster innovation, higher local relevance	Greater variation in delivery, oversight complexity

Lever	Benefit	Trade-Off
Peer moderation systems	Higher trust, more ownership	Risk of uneven standards
Partner self-service tools	Lower overhead, scalable partnerships	Quality control and alignment risks
Curated content ecosystems	Better matching, community insight	Requires investment in tagging, feedback, curation logic

Linking Transaction Costs to ROI

Reducing transaction costs directly affects platform performance and financial logic. It:

- Improves Return on Platform Investment (ROPI) by reducing coordination overhead
- Unlocks latent member contributions by reducing engagement friction
- Strengthens network effects by increasing trust and ease of participation

In short, every unit of friction removed increases platform yield.

Platform-in-Practice: Governance Streamlining at AEC

The Allied Education Council (AEC)[2] faced a 12-month cycle to update core curricula due to overlapping committees and legacy sign-off rules. After a governance redesign, it:

- Created a *design sandbox* for pilots
- Delegated authority to time-bound advisory panels
- Used member review to refine content before final board endorsement
- Curriculum update time dropped to 90 days. Member engagement rose. Transaction costs didn't vanish, they were *redistributed for speed, inclusion, and trust.*

The Boardroom Shift:

When the association's board reviewed the strategy retreat outputs, the Chair summarised the shift:

"We've been asking, 'What should we do more of?' But maybe the better question is, 'What are we making harder than it needs to be?'"

Reducing transaction costs is not just an efficiency play. It's a strategic redesign of how your association coordinates trust, enables participation, and governs value.

Because in platform economies, the winners aren't the ones who do the most, they're the ones who enable others to do more, with less friction.

---

[2] We use demonstration cases rather than real scenarios due to the issues of confidentiality and the lack of good examples.

Next, we explore another overlooked force that shapes economic design and legitimacy: *externalities*, the unpriced impacts associations create (or absorb) as they scale.

Platform-in-Practice: Member CPD Marketplace

A national professional body launched a new digital CPD platform. At first, it centralised all course listings, approvals, and quality checks through its internal education team.

But friction emerged:

- Members struggled to find relevant content tailored to their specialisation or location
- External content partners waited months for approval
- The education team became a bottleneck, juggling reviews, updates, and support tickets

A transaction cost audit revealed high search, decision, and enforcement costs. The platform was reliable, but slow and opaque.

The solution?

- Introduce member tagging and rating for CPD modules
- Enable pre-approved partners to self-publish within clear quality parameters
- Add automated prompts and filters to help members discover personalised pathways

Result: Member satisfaction improved, partner onboarding accelerated, and the education team shifted to strategic curation instead of micromanagement.

Insight: Streamlining doesn't mean reducing standards, it means designing workflows that distribute trust and decision-making more intelligently.

Platform-in-Practice: Friction in Advocacy Coordination

A health peak body coordinated member consultation for national policy submissions. Every round involved:

- Dozens of email threads
- Multiple briefing papers rewritten for each sub-sector
- Long review cycles across state chapters
- A final rush to synthesise everything before submission deadlines

Despite goodwill and commitment, participants described the process as exhausting and inefficient. A classic case of decision and enforcement transaction costs.

The association introduced a collaborative policy wiki with:

- Shared versioning, sector-tagged contribution threads
- Real-time moderation by policy staff
- A live "insight tracker" dashboard highlighting consensus and contention

The result was faster, more inclusive, and more transparent policy generation, with higher engagement from younger members who previously opted out of slow governance processes.

Platform-in-Practice: Sponsorship Complexity at Scale

An education-focused association relied on relationship managers to negotiate sponsorships. As the partner base grew, so did the problems:

- Inconsistent pricing
- Delayed contract cycles
- Custom packages that were difficult to track or deliver
- Staff turnover caused loss of sponsor context and trust

Transaction cost analysis revealed high bargaining and enforcement friction.

The solution?

- Develop a tiered, self-service sponsorship portal with templated packages and calendar-based inventory
- Automate compliance tracking and activation deliverables
- Use shared dashboards for internal delivery teams and sponsors

The partner experience improved, staff capacity was freed up, and sponsorship revenue stabilised without additional headcount.

Platform-in-Practice: Volunteer Fatigue as Transaction Cost Burnout

In a federation-style association, each chapter operated semi-autonomously. Volunteer leaders coordinated events, managed mailing lists, and organised CPD with minimal support.

Over time, volunteers dropped off. New ones didn't step up. The reason? The "workload" wasn't the problem, coordination friction was.

The national office redesigned the platform:

- Rolled out shared tooling (templates, scheduling platforms, email automation)
- Centralised registration and payment processing
- Offered optional event-in-a-box packs with customisation options
- Delegated authority through fast-track approval pathways

Result: Volunteer satisfaction rose. Participation rebounded. Transaction costs were redistributed, away from ad hoc administration and toward strategic community-building.

Chapter 4. Externalities

The Impacts You Don't Price and Why They Matter More Than You Think

Three months after the retreat, the association's new digital credentialing pilot was up and running. Member uptake was strong. Feedback positive. The platform was humming.

But during a routine board meeting, a quiet question broke the rhythm.

"*Has anyone thought about the public impact of all this?*" asked the Ethics Committee Chair. "*We're issuing credentials that employers now treat as standard, but what happens when non-members are excluded?*"

The room paused.

The pilot had been built for efficiency. But no one had mapped its externalities.

What Are Externalities?

In economics, an externality is a cost or benefit that arises from a transaction but isn't paid or received by the parties directly involved. Instead, it is 'externalised' and imposed on others.

- **Positive externalities**: Benefits spill over. *Example,* An association publishes open standards that improve sector performance.
- **Negative externalities**: Harms go unaccounted. *Example,* An association's sponsored webinar spreads misinformation or marginalises small providers.

Most associations don't set out to create negative externalities. But platform scale introduces complexity and complexity makes unintended consequences more likely.

Externalities in Associations: Common Types

Table 4-1 Externalities in Associations

Type	Examples in the Association Context
Informational	Misinformation spreads via partner content or low-quality forums
Cultural/Access-Based	Credentialing systems unintentionally exclude diverse learners
Governance	Sponsorship influence distorts strategic priorities
Reputational	Affiliation with unethical providers damages brand trust
Public Good Underinvestment	Data or insights are locked behind paywalls, reducing sector innovation

Associations are often caught between two roles: serving members and stewarding public trust. Externalities sit at that intersection. They are the unpriced costs or unclaimed benefits of how associations operate, scale, and govern.

Example: The CPD Accreditation Externality

Consider an association that builds a Continuing Professional Development (CPD) accreditation platform to approve learning providers and list endorsed programs. The goal is to ensure quality and consistency for members.

Intended outcome: Members access trusted learning experiences; providers gain visibility.

But over time:

- Only well-funded providers can afford the accreditation fee and meet complex requirements.
- Smaller community-led programs are excluded due to lack of formal credentialing.
- Employers begin using the association's list as a proxy for job readiness.

Externalities created:

- Negative cultural externality: The system unintentionally marginalises culturally diverse or grassroots training providers.
- Governance externality: The association becomes a de facto gatekeeper of legitimacy, without being mandated to do so.
- Reputational externality: Excluded providers criticise the system publicly, harming the association's perceived neutrality.

Positive counterpoint: If the association adjusted its model to subsidise small providers or recognise alternative credentials, it could generate positive access externalities, improving inclusion and sector diversity.

Takeaway: Even well-meaning platforms can create invisible governance footprints. Externalities often arise from how associations scale, not just what they intend.

Why Governance Must Care

Here's the danger: Platform economics makes it easy to grow without noticing what you're growing. Without mechanisms to detect impact, price unaccounted costs, and reinvest value beyond direct transactions, associations risk undermining their own legitimacy, even as their services become more sophisticated. Governance must play an active role in monitoring, managing, and, where necessary, redistributing the effects of association activity.

Designing for Externality Governance

Leading platform-based associations are starting to think like public stewards as well as strategic designers.

Table 4-2 Designing for Eternality Governance

Governance Mechanism	How It Addresses Externalities
Open data and standards	Shares sectoral value beyond membership walls
Equity audits	Detects who benefits (and who doesn't) from new initiatives
Ethics panels or peer councils	Reviews impact of partner programs and content pipelines
Distributed moderation	Manages misinformation or exclusion in peer-led communities
Impact metrics (not just KPIs)	Tracks unintended effects across members, partners, and the public

This is not about perfection, it's about intentionality. The question isn't whether your association creates externalities. The question is whether you're governing them.

Case Study: Meta-Governance for Privacy, Stewarding Civic *Trust through Institutional Design*

Could a hypothetical Australian professional association recognise that its privacy governance framework, anchored in compliance checklists and risk disclosures, and was no longer fit for purpose? If it treated privacy as a compliance risk, not as a strategic governance domain. It ignored the relational, systemic, and legitimacy aspects of privacy in a networked association model, particularly where platform partnerships, data ecosystems, and civic expectations intersect, then it should. In response, it could adopt a meta-governance approach, shifting from individual consent mechanisms toward institutional stewardship grounded in relational legitimacy.

The Trigger: Following concerns from members about opaque data use in CPD platforms and third-party webinar partnerships, the board commissioned an equity and privacy audit. The findings revealed that despite adherence to regulatory obligations, the association had unintentionally facilitated informational externalities (e.g. user data used for commercial profiling) and cultural externalities (e.g. marginalisation of members with limited digital literacy or access).

The Shift: Rather than respond with tighter controls or member disclaimers, the association redefined privacy as a civic value, not a compliance artefact. It embraced meta-governance principles:

- Establishing a cross-functional Privacy Stewardship Committee including board members, members, technologists, and ethics advisors.
- Co-designing a participatory oversight mechanism, a Civic Panel to review the impact of new digital offerings before launch.
- Publishing open impact dashboards that report on trust metrics, data usage transparency, and feedback from underrepresented member cohorts.

The Outcome: Within 12 months, the association aimed to:

- Reduced reliance on partner data brokers
- Embedded privacy by governance into all digital procurement frameworks
- Demonstrated measurable improvements in Net Positive Engagement and member trust scores
- Contributed to sector-wide discussions on anticipatory ethics and platform accountability
- Increase membership engagement as their "trust bank" increased.

Lesson: By treating privacy failures not merely as legal risks but as negative externalities affecting its broader public role, the association reframed its governance from defensive posture to civic stewardship. The result was a more coherent alignment between strategy, trust, and public legitimacy, illustrating how platform-based associations can govern externalities through intentional design rather than after-the-fact mitigation.

The Deeper Insight: Purpose Without Price Is Not Enough

Back in the boardroom, the Chair concluded the meeting with a reflection:

> *"We keep talking about purpose. But if we're not designing for impact, or pricing the harm we pass on, we're not living it."*

In a platform-shaped world, economic thinking is ethical thinking. Externalities are where trust lives or dies. And for associations whose brand rests on legitimacy, inclusion, and shared value, that makes externalities not an afterthought, but a board-level responsibility.

What Comes Next

With these three concepts, network effects, transaction costs, and externalities, we now have the economic lens through which association performance, value creation, and governance maturity can be meaningfully reimagined.

In the next chapter, we introduce a structured framework to help association leaders use this lens strategically: the Platform Design Levers, a set of economic and operational variables that leaders can pull to design for value, scale, and trust in complex ecosystems.

Summary: What Every Association Board Should Understand

1. Multi-Sided Platforms Are the New Default

Associations increasingly operate as multi-sided platforms, enabling interaction between members, learners, employers, partners, and sponsors. Value no longer flows linearly from provider to member. It emerges through participation, network connections, and governance of exchange.

2. Network Effects Drive Scalable Value

The more people who interact meaningfully through your platform, the more valuable it becomes, for everyone. But network effects must be designed, not assumed. Friction, silos, or one-way delivery models kill them.

3. Transaction Costs Are Your Hidden Budget

Search, coordination, and enforcement costs drain energy, time, and value, especially when decision-making is slow or infrastructure is clunky. Platform models require new ways to manage these costs through design, delegation, and technology.

4. Externalities Shape Reputation and Relevance

Every association creates effects beyond its direct transactions, for good or ill. If you don't govern them, you risk unintentionally excluding, misleading, or losing trust. Externality stewardship is now a *core governance function,* not a compliance bolt-on.

5. Economic Design Is a Leadership Responsibility

This isn't just about finance or digital teams. It's a board-level shift. To lead in a platform era, association directors and executives must understand, and actively shape, the *economic architecture* of value creation, participation, and trust.

PART II Economic Foundations for Platform-Based Associations

This section brings together the economic logic, financial modelling tools, governance diagnostics, and analytical methods that underpin platform success in the association sector. While earlier chapters explored strategy, governance, and capability-building, this part equips association leaders with the economic and structural frameworks needed to make confident, data-driven decisions.

As associations evolve from service providers to platform orchestrators, the economics of scale, value creation, and revenue design also change. These chapters offer board-ready guidance and theoretical rigour to help decision-makers manage that shift.

Chapter 5. Economics of Engagement

From Services to Systems of Contribution

In the legacy association model, value was produced internally and consumed externally. Staff designed the products, set the calendar, delivered the benefits. Members paid, attended, and received.

Platform-based associations flip this logic. Here, value emerges from systems of interaction, not just services. Members are not passive recipients but active participants. And every interaction, posting a job, mentoring a peer, attending an event, contributing data, becomes part of a living economic system.

Understanding this transformation requires a new economic lens: one that focuses not only on what the association *delivers*, but on how value is *created, shared, and scaled* across a network.

From Calendar-Based Delivery to Ecosystem-Driven Value

Legacy Model, Event Delivery Approach

The National Marketing Association (NMA)[3] historically operated on a membership value model centred around an annual calendar of events. Staff curated topics, sourced speakers, booked venues, and handled registrations. Members paid annual dues and attended events to receive updates, earn CPD points, or network. Value was delivered by the organisation and consumed by members. The interaction was largely one-directional, and success was measured by attendance numbers and satisfaction surveys.

Platform-Based Model, Ecosystem Participation Approach

As part of a strategic transformation, NMA restructured its operations around a member participation platform. Instead of simply delivering content, it enabled members to co-create value through a digital and relational ecosystem. Features included:

- A peer-to-peer mentoring exchange, where members could both offer and request guidance based on areas of expertise
- A job board that not only listed vacancies but also allowed members to signal interest in secondments, projects, or cross-sector collaborations
- Micro-credential pathways built from member-contributed case studies and use cases, linked to discussion forums and real-time peer ratings
- A data dashboard that showed live insights drawn from member input, such as salary benchmarks, campaign metrics, and industry trends

In this platform model, NMA no longer simply delivers a service. It curates, facilitates, and governs a system of interactions. Each action, mentoring, sharing data, posting opportunities, contributing feedback, becomes a node in a living economic network. The

---

[3] This is a demonstration example only.

association's role shifts from producer to orchestrator, and its governance must now support trust, participation, and interoperability, not just event logistics.

Economic Implication

This transformation reframes value not as a product, but as a flow. It demands a new economic lens that can evaluate participation intensity, feedback loops, network externalities, and trust as economic assets. The association's success is measured not only by what it delivers, but by the volume, diversity, and coherence of value creation across the network.

Rethinking Value: From Delivery to Enablement

The conventional logic of value in associations is based on provision: services are bundled, priced (typically via membership fees), and delivered.

But in a platform-enabled association, the role shifts from provider to enabler. The association's economic logic becomes *interactional*, not transactional.

Table 5-1 Rethinking Value

Legacy Model	Platform Model
Value is created by staff	Value is co-created by users and partners
Focus on delivery	Focus on enablement
Cost-based pricing	Outcome-based value creation
Passive consumption	Participatory contribution

Designing for Participation: The Economics of Contribution

In platform-based associations, value is not created solely by what the organisation delivers. It is generated through what members contribute, their time, insight, data, content, and feedback. Contribution becomes the core economic engine of the platform. A platform thrives when participation is active, meaningful, and scalable.

However, not all contributions carry equal weight, and participation is not guaranteed. Associations must intentionally design systems that encourage, reward, and sustain member contribution.

Key economic design levers include:

- **Reciprocity:** Members are more likely to contribute when they perceive mutual benefit. Peer mentoring is a prime example, where both parties receive value through shared learning and support.
- **Reputation:** Recognition mechanisms, such as contributor badges, curated profiles, or featured content, build status and credibility. These systems reward valued behaviours and reinforce continued engagement.
- **Access:** Contributions can unlock deeper layers of the platform experience. This might include access to premium content, eligibility for leadership roles, or influence in governance processes. When participation creates opportunity, the platform becomes a ladder, not just a service.

- **Network Utility:** The more others participate, the more valuable each individual interaction becomes. This is the principle of network effects. A discussion forum with ten active contributors is more useful than one with two. A credentialing pathway co-developed by diverse members holds more relevance and legitimacy.

This is where the line between economic design and governance design begins to blur. Rules shape incentives, and incentives shape participation. Governance determines who can act, how contributions are recognised, and what behaviours are rewarded or restricted.

Designing for participation requires a careful balance between openness and structure, between individual motivation and collective value. When done well, it transforms members from passive recipients into active co-creators, turning the association into a dynamic, self-reinforcing system of shared value.

Case Example: Designing a Peer Contribution Ladder

The *Professional Network Association (PNA)*[4] launched a new platform-based CPD ecosystem, aimed at shifting its role from content distributor to ecosystem enabler. Early usage data revealed a pattern: while members consumed large volumes of content, very few contributed back. Webinars lacked interactivity, forums were stagnant, and course reviews were sparse. The platform's value was plateauing.

To address this, PNA redesigned the system around the *economics of contribution*, applying four key design levers:

1. Reciprocity Engine: Peer Mentoring Circles

Members could opt in as mentors or mentees. But instead of treating this as a one-way relationship, the system embedded two-way benefits:

- Mentors received CPD credits and early access to upcoming leadership masterclasses.
- Mentees could nominate mentors for 'Most Impactful Contributor' badges, which carried visible status in member profiles.

Result: Mentors reported gaining new insights from mentees, flipping the dynamic from unidirectional expertise-sharing to mutual enrichment.

2. Reputation and Recognition: Contributor Profiles

PNA introduced dynamic contributor profiles showing:

- Articles or toolkits authored
- Community responses to posts (e.g. 'Most Helpful' tags)
- Micro-credentials earned for facilitation or peer support

---

4 Professional Network Association (PNA) was the demonstration cases used in The Modern Association Playbook.

- High-reputation contributors were featured in the monthly 'Member Spotlight' and offered the opportunity to co-develop future content series.

3. Access Pathways: Tiered Participation Incentives

Instead of gating content by payment, PNA introduced *contribution tiers:*

- *Explorer*: Free access to standard content
- *Collaborator*: Earned by submitting reviews or responding in forums—unlocked member-only datasets and tools
- *Builder*: Gained access to content co-design teams, advisory panels, and discounted leadership retreats

This positioned contribution as a pathway, not a burden, and gave members agency in shaping the platform's evolution.

4. Network Utility: Designing for Density

To accelerate participation, PNA seeded ten active contributors into each learning forum at launch, ensuring early discussions had depth and responsiveness. This created an initial feedback loop that amplified network value.

They also clustered contributions visually by topic heatmaps, so members could see where activity was concentrated, nudging them into richer dialogue spaces.

Boardroom Insight

PNA didn't just reward activity. It redefined participation as a value-generating asset. By aligning reciprocity, reputation, access, and network effects, the platform evolved from a library to a living system, where contribution became the economic fuel and governance, the engine of trust.

Mapping Value Flows Across the Platform

A successful platform does not simply deliver value. It enables value to flow between participants. To build a robust and sustainable platform model, associations must understand where value originates, how it moves between actors, where it accumulates, and how it is sustained over time.

This requires a shift from a linear view of value creation to a systems perspective. In a platform context, value is exchanged, amplified, and redistributed across multiple sides. The association's role is to govern and facilitate these flows, ensuring that exchanges are efficient, trusted, and aligned with shared purpose.

Example: Mapping a Multi-Sided Association Platform

Consider a typical professional association that connects members, corporate partners, educators, and regulators.

The platform does not create all of this value directly. Instead, it supports interactions between participants by removing barriers, increasing visibility, and building trust. It operates as a facilitator of value exchange rather than a sole producer. By mapping these value flows, associations can identify strengths and gaps in their ecosystem.

Table 5-2 Mapping Flows

Group	Inputs	Value Received
Members	Fees, feedback, content, peer support	CPD, reputation, networking, influence
Corporate Partners	Sponsorship, jobs, datasets	Brand, recruitment access, insights
Educators	Content, credentials, learning pathways	Recognition, reach, learner engagement
Regulators	Policy alignment, standards input	Access to sector data, legitimacy support

This understanding can guide strategic decisions, highlight areas for governance attention, and improve the overall alignment between contributors and beneficiaries. Knowing where value enters and where it accumulates is essential for platform sustainability. It allows the association to invest in the relationships, processes, and tools that make the system work at scale.

Designing for Incentive Alignment

One of the major challenges in platform design is preventing value leakage. This occurs when participants benefit from the platform without contributing meaningfully, or when governance structures unintentionally discourage engagement. Free-riding, low participation, and incentive mismatches can undermine the sustainability of the platform and weaken the trust of active contributors.

To manage this risk, associations must take a proactive design approach. This includes:

- **Defining who creates value and who receives it**: Understanding the role of each participant group is critical. Not all members contribute in the same way, and not all benefits are equally distributed.
- **Ensuring value creators receive appropriate returns**: Those who contribute time, knowledge, data, or leadership should experience tangible and recognised benefits. This may include visibility, influence, access, or direct reciprocity.
- **Designing rules that reinforce contribution, not just compliance**: Governance frameworks should reward constructive participation. This includes embedding incentives in program structures, eligibility criteria, or access pathways that favour active engagement over passive consumption.

A practical tool to support this analysis is the *Contribution–Incentive Alignment Matrix*. This tool helps assess whether each group's contributions are matched with meaningful incentives and whether any misalignments are creating friction, discouragement, or strategic risk.

Table 5-3 Contribution–Incentive Alignment Matrix

User Group	Primary Contribution	Value Received	Incentive Type	Alignment Rating 1 to 5	Comments / Gaps
Members	Time, fees, feedback, peer support, event participation	CPD, networking, recognition, influence	Reputation, reciprocity		Are active contributors recognised distinctly?
Mentors / Volunteers	Expertise, guidance, community-building	Visibility, influence, professional development	Reputation, access		Do you track and reward this work explicitly?
Corporate Partners	Sponsorship, data, recruitment channels	Brand exposure, access to members, policy visibility	Commercial, influence		Is partner engagement driving mutual outcomes?
Educators / Experts	Content creation, credential development	Platform visibility, reach, credential uptake	Visibility, authority		Are they incentivised to innovate / update?
New Contributors	Questions, feedback, early interactions	Access, onboarding experience, social capital	Reciprocity, access		Are entry points low-friction and rewarding?
Lurkers / Passive Users	Minimal or no contribution	Full access to services or reputation benefits	Free-riding		Is the model tolerating unreciprocated access?

Economic Models of Engagement: Freemium, Tiered Access, and Participation Currency

As presented in *The Modern Association Playbook*, traditional membership tiers in many associations are struggling to keep pace with how members actually engage and contribute. Static fee-for-access models often misalign with modern expectations, leaving highly engaged contributors under-recognised while low-participation members continue to receive full benefits. This creates inefficiencies in value allocation and weakens incentives for sustained participation.

Platform economics offers a more flexible and responsive set of engagement models. These models shift the economic logic from a purely transactional arrangement to one based on interaction, contribution, and dynamic exchange.

Three emerging models are particularly relevant for association platforms:

- **Freemium Models:** Inspired by digital platforms, the freemium model allows open access to base-level services while reserving advanced tools, insights, or opportunities for those who upgrade or contribute more. For associations, this might include open access to newsletters and basic forums, with premium features such as job boards, benchmarking dashboards, or advanced analytics reserved for contributors or paying members. This approach reduces barriers to entry while still generating value from high-demand features.
- **Tiered Participation Models:** Rather than tying access to a fixed membership tier, this model links engagement levels to actual contribution. For example, a member who regularly mentors others, contributes to content development, or moderates discussions might gain access to exclusive forums, event discounts, or co-design opportunities. This approach aligns value distribution with member activity, not just financial commitment.
- **Tokenised or Participation Currency Models:** Conceptually drawn from digital and cooperative systems, this model allows members to earn non-monetary credits based on their contributions. These credits can be redeemed for tangible or intangible benefits such as event access, professional development opportunities, governance roles, or digital recognition. While still in early stages for most associations, this model offers a promising direction for incentivising meaningful participation and reinforcing community norms.

Each of these models reframes engagement not as a static entitlement but as a dynamic, ongoing exchange. Instead of paying to receive, members are invited to participate, contribute, and shape the value they experience. This transition supports greater equity, scalability, and adaptability within the platform economy.

From an economic perspective, these models:

- Improve alignment between value creation and value receipt
- Reduce participation barriers, especially for early-career or underrepresented members
- Encourage ongoing involvement through non-financial incentives
- Enable more granular tracking of engagement patterns and community health

Associations that adopt these models must also update their governance frameworks accordingly. Transparent rules, fair attribution systems, and trust-enhancing design are essential to ensure these models are legitimate, ethical, and widely embraced.

The Risk of Misalignment: Value Without Flow

Platform associations rely on continuous value flow between participants. When this flow is disrupted or poorly designed, the result is misalignment, a condition where the association extracts contributions without adequately returning value, distributes benefits inequitably, or concentrates decision-making in ways that inhibit trust and engagement.

Without a clear value architecture, associations risk falling into patterns that may feel cultural, but are in fact structural and economic in nature. Common symptoms of misalignment include:

- **Contributor fatigue:** When members consistently contribute time, knowledge, or content without visible recognition or benefit, motivation declines. The platform becomes extractive rather than generative, and contributors may disengage entirely.
- **Governance gridlock or compaction:** When decisions are concentrated at the board/executive level, and participation pathways are unclear or tokenistic, members lack influence. This slows down innovation, increases internal friction, and reduces the platform's ability to adapt.
- **Perceived inequity:** If highly engaged contributors and minimally active members receive the same benefits, this creates resentment and weakens community cohesion. Over time, this erodes the value of participation and discourages deeper involvement.

These are not simply cultural or operational problems. They are indicators of flawed economic and governance design. When value does not flow in proportion to contribution, trust breaks down. When governance does not reflect the structure of participation, alignment is lost.

The consequences are tangible. Associations may experience:

- Lower member retention and renewal rates
- Increased internal tension between volunteer leaders and staff
- Difficulty scaling or sustaining platform initiatives

- Strategic drift, where engagement models no longer match mission or market

Avoiding these risks requires intentional design. Value must be mapped, flows must be governed, and engagement must be supported through aligned economic and governance mechanisms. When done well, the result is not only a more vibrant platform, but a more resilient and trusted institution.

Economic Architecture as Strategic Infrastructure

In a platform association, *value architecture* is not a secondary concern. It is strategic infrastructure. Just like roads enable transport, pipes carry water, or code runs a digital platform, value architecture determines how participation, recognition, trust, and resources move through the system.

Economic architecture shapes what flows where, who contributes and who benefits, what incentives are activated, and how outcomes are distributed. It is the underlying structure that determines whether the association operates as a cohesive ecosystem or a fragmented network.

To build effective infrastructure for value creation and exchange, platform-based associations must:

- **Map user groups, contribution systems, and value flows:** This includes understanding the roles of different stakeholders, the kinds of contributions they make, and how these generate or sustain value across the platform.
- **Identify blockages, leakages, and imbalances:** Blockages might include underused participation pathways or restricted access. Leakages occur when value is extracted without reciprocal contribution. Imbalances may show up when some groups benefit disproportionately to what they contribute.
- **Adjust design rules to optimise system performance:** This might involve introducing new participation models, refining incentive structures, revising pricing tiers, or reconfiguring governance arrangements that affect decision rights and benefit allocation.

A well-designed economic architecture ensures that value flows are not accidental or arbitrary. Instead, they are purposefully structured to support fairness, efficiency, and strategic alignment.

Ultimately, associations that treat value architecture as infrastructure are better positioned to adapt, scale, and maintain trust. They are able to build ecosystems where members, partners, and other stakeholders contribute willingly and benefit meaningfully, not because they are told to, but because the system makes it worthwhile.

Example: When Contribution Outpaces Recognition – A Misalignment Story

Context:

The *Australian Professional Educators Network (APEN)*[5] launched a knowledge-sharing platform designed to crowdsource lesson plans, classroom strategies, and peer-to-peer mentoring for early career teachers. The idea was simple: harness the insight of experienced educators and share it with the next generation.

Initial uptake was promising. Within months, hundreds of lesson resources were uploaded, and mentoring sessions had begun to scale. But by the second year, participation started to decline. Key contributors stopped submitting content. Mentors pulled out of programs. Forum activity dropped sharply.

Diagnosis:

What looked like cultural disengagement turned out to be structural misalignment.

- **Contributor fatigue:** APEN had failed to introduce recognition or feedback loops for the most active contributors. Experienced educators who donated hours of content received no analytics, no credit, and no professional benefit beyond personal satisfaction.
- **Governance compaction:** Strategic decisions about platform direction, partner content, and funding allocations were made centrally, with no advisory role for the most active platform users. Contributor voices were absent from governance.
- **Perceived inequity:** All users, regardless of activity level, received equal platform access and benefits. Highly engaged members saw their work repackaged in branded outputs without attribution, while passive members consumed resources freely.

Consequences:

Monthly active contributors dropped significantly.

- Several high-profile early adopters left the community and publicly criticised the model.
- Sponsorships declined, citing unclear value metrics and declining engagement.
- Internal staff struggled to pivot due to lack of contributor trust and involvement in redesign efforts.

Strategic Response:

APEN initiated a *value flow audit*. This included:

- Mapping contributor journeys and feedback loops
- Interviewing top contributors to understand pain points
- Identifying where value was being extracted without return

---

5 Demonstration only.

Redesign Measures:

- Introduced a *Contribution Equity Model*: Active contributors received tiered recognition badges, access to exclusive content, and early invitations to co-create resources.
- Established a *Contributor Advisory Board* with direct input into platform features and partner relationships.
- Added dashboards showing contribution impact (downloads, shares, ratings) to help educators demonstrate professional value.
- Adjusted licensing and attribution protocols so educators retained credit and optional copyright over their content.

Boardroom Reflection

This was not a case of "burnout" or "bad engagement". It was economic misalignment. The platform's architecture failed to return value in proportion to contribution.

Engagement is Economic Design

In a platform-based association, engagement is no longer a soft or secondary metric. It is an economic outcome, shaped by structural design choices. Participation does not happen by accident. It is a contribution that responds to incentives, governance settings, and value flows within a shared system.

This chapter has outlined how associations can move beyond transactional models by building economic infrastructure that supports:

- Meaningful contribution
- Sustained interaction
- Aligned and transparent incentives across stakeholders

When participation is designed as a core element of the platform economy, engagement becomes measurable, scalable, and strategically valuable.

The next chapter shifts focus from participation to monetisation. It explores how these design principles can be translated into revenue models that are mission-aligned, ethically priced, and built for long-term resilience. Engagement and income are not separate concerns. They are part of the same economic system, one that associations must learn to govern intentionally.

Summary: Economics of Engagement

1. Engagement is Economic, Not Just Behavioural

In platform associations, engagement is not just member satisfaction, it's a form of value creation and contribution. Every interaction is an economic act that must be supported by appropriate design levers.

2. Value Emerges Through Participation

Platform logic shifts associations from content delivery to interaction enablement. Members, partners, and contributors co-create value, and the association must design the conditions for that value to scale.

3. Incentives Drive Contribution

Reciprocity, reputation, access, and network utility are the levers that drive sustained participation. Without aligned incentives, contributions stall, fatigue sets in, and ecosystems fracture.

4. Mapping Value Flows Is Strategic Infrastructure

Value doesn't just originate with the association, it flows through users, partners, educators, and sponsors. Associations must understand who gives, who benefits, and how to close the loop.

5. Misalignment Is a Design Failure, Not a User Problem

If high contributors receive the same returns as passive users, engagement will erode. Value leakage, perceived inequity, and contributor churn are symptoms of broken economic architecture.

6. Engagement Strategy = Incentive Architecture + Governance Logic

Economic engagement design must be embedded in pricing, platforms, recognition systems, and governance rules. Strategy is not what you say, it's how your structure makes people behave.

Chapter 6. Platform-Enhanced Business Model Canvas

This mini-chapter is inserted here to set you up for the next chapters.

A Strategic Design Tool for Mapping Participation, Value, and Trust

As associations shift from product-based delivery to platform-enabled coordination, traditional business planning tools are showing their limits. Standard models often fail to capture the complexity of modern associations, where value is co-created across diverse user groups, governance is distributed, and legitimacy is as important as revenue.

This chapter introduces the Platform-Enhanced Business Model Canvas: a strategic tool adapted from Osterwalder's original framework but tailored for the economic logic of platform-based associations. It reflects the transition outlined in earlier chapters, from linear delivery to interactional value creation, from cost-recovery models to network-enabled ecosystems.

Why Boards Need a New Canvas

This business model canvas is not just a facilitation tool. It's a governance instrument.

- It maps where value is created, and by whom
- It highlights where participation friction may stall engagement
- It links revenue generation with trust dynamics and reputational risk
- It reveals misalignments between strategic goals and platform infrastructure

For boards stewarding a shift toward *The Modern Association Playbook's* Association 2.0 or 3.0 models, this canvas supports strategic clarity, risk foresight, and ethical oversight, especially where decisions about monetisation, participation, or partnerships are complex or contested.

The *Platform-Enhanced Business Model Canvas* adapts the well-known Business Model Canvas for the unique context of platform-based associations. It incorporates additional layers relevant to participation, trust, governance, and risk, enabling boards and executive teams to better align their economic architecture with platform logic.

Where the legacy model focused on linear value delivery, this canvas highlights how value emerges from interaction, how different participant groups contribute and benefit, and where governance design influences both monetisation and legitimacy. It encourages associations to think in terms of systems, not silos, mapping how strategic choices in one part of the model affect trust, sustainability, and performance in others.

This canvas is designed to be used in:

- Strategic workshops and board planning sessions
- Revenue model design and diversification initiatives
- Governance and risk reviews
- Co-design processes with key stakeholder groups

Table 6-1 outlines each area of the canvas, followed by a worked example and practical guidance on how to apply it.

Table 6-1 Platform-Enhanced Business Model Canvas

Canvas Area	Modified Focus	Strategic Prompt
Participant Segments	Multi-sided actors	Who are the key groups engaging with our platform (e.g. members, partners, employers, learners)?
Value Propositions	Multi-actor value	What value does each participant group receive or create? How does this value emerge?
Participation Pathways	Interaction channels	How do participants connect, contribute, and access value (e.g. portal, events, forums, co-design groups)?
Relationships & Trust	Trust, reciprocity, transparency	How do we build credibility, ethical governance, and engagement across diverse actors?
Revenue Streams	Actor-specific monetisation	How is revenue generated from or through each actor group? Is it direct, indirect, or blended?
Key Contributions	From members and partners	What do participants contribute (e.g. content, data, facilitation, reputation)? How is this supported and recognised?
Key Resources	Platform + relational infrastructure	What capabilities (tech, data, staff, systems) are required to support interactions and value creation?
Key Partnerships	Ecosystem and enablers	Who do we partner with to expand our impact (e.g. EdTech, government, industry, funders)?
Cost Structure	Operational, relational, governance	What are the core costs? Which costs are fixed vs variable? Where does governance effort sit?
Governance & Ethics (New)	Oversight, inclusion, safeguards	How is the platform governed? Who has voice and decision rights? How is data used and protected?
Risk & Reputational Zones (New)	Potential friction points	What parts of the model could backfire (e.g. paywalls, data use, partner alignment)? What safeguards are in place?

Worked Example: PNA's CPD and Career Services Platform

Table 6-2 Worked Example: PNA's CPD and Career Services Platform

Canvas Area	Example from PNA
Participant Segments	Early-career professionals, experienced members, mentors, employers, CPD partners
Value Propositions	Members gain CPD, networking, and career pathways; partners access a skills-aligned audience; mentors gain recognition and leadership exposure
Participation Pathways	Member portal with CPD dashboard, peer-learning circles, mentoring forums, job board
Relationships & Trust	Transparent recognition of contributions; open member feedback loop; consent-based data use
Revenue Streams	Premium membership tiers; micro-credential fees; employer partnerships; CPD partner licensing
Key Contributions	Members contribute lived experience (e.g. case studies), co-lead webinars, participate in peer-review
Key Resources	Modular LMS, CRM-integrated member portal, CPD credentialing framework, facilitation staff
Key Partnerships	Universities (micro-credential co-design), tech providers (platform stack), employers (job placement)
Cost Structure	Platform licensing, content development, governance costs (e.g. ethics review panel), staff time for moderation and support
Governance & Ethics	Board-approved Monetisation Charter; co-designed CPD standards; member advisory panel on pricing
Risk & Reputational Zones	Paywall backlash if essential CPD is locked; data use concerns; partner credibility risks, all mitigated by phased piloting and ethical review processes

How to Use This Canvas

- Board Strategy Workshops: Use this as a boardroom tool to map current vs proposed business models.
- Revenue Planning: Align proposed monetisation strategies with participant value and trust dynamics.
- Governance Oversight: Spot friction points and pre-empt reputational risks.
- Pilot Design: Choose one actor group and co-design with them first before scaling.

How to Use This Canvas Strategically

This tool is designed to help association leaders translate platform economics into board-level strategy. It can be used in the following contexts:

Table 6-3 Using the Canvas

Use Case	Application
Board Strategy Retreats	Map your current vs target model, especially during digital transformation
Revenue Model Review	Ensure alignment between monetisation mechanisms, participation pathways, and trust dynamics
Governance and Risk Review	Identify points of ethical tension or design strain (e.g. participation exclusion, partner risk)
Co-Design with Stakeholders	Involve a key actor group in mapping value flows and testing assumptions before scaling
Platform ROI Planning	Use canvas inputs to feed into tools like the *ROPI Model* (Chapter 8), pricing diagnostics, or friction audits

Integrating Canvas with APSF and Governance Diagnostics

The Platform-Enhanced Canvas can serve as a **bridge tool** between your high-level strategy (via the Association Platform Success Framework) and your more granular diagnostics (e.g. Governance Alignment Grid, Participation Cost Index, or ROPI).

For example:

- Use the Participation Pathways area to inform APSF pillar mapping
- Link Revenue Streams and Value Propositions to the *Monetisation Decision Matrix*
- Connect Governance & Ethics and Risk Zones to friction diagnostics from *Chapter 12*

Final Prompt: What Is Your Association Really Built to Do?

Traditional business models describe what an organisation offers and how it earns revenue. But platform associations must go deeper. They must understand:

- Who they serve and how they interact
- What kinds of value are being exchanged
- How governance either enables or constrains participation
- Where trust is won, or lost

This canvas is not just a planning tool. It's a mirror. And what it reveals can help your association move from activity to architecture, from engagement to enablement, and from service provider to platform steward.

See Chapter 19 for more insights.

Part III: Strategic Modelling for Monetisation and Value Exchange

Designing Economic Architecture for Sustainable Platform Associations

Platform-era associations cannot rely on legacy revenue streams, passive membership dues, or episodic sponsorship. To thrive, they must intentionally design for value exchange, and monetise it ethically, adaptively, and with strategic clarity.

This section moves from theory to design. It explores how associations can model participation as an economic engine, not just a communications challenge, and how to align monetisation strategies with trust, mission, and member outcomes.

We examine the levers of value creation in a platform context: segmentation, contribution loops, network dynamics, and incentive structures. We challenge conventional revenue thinking and offer a portfolio approach to monetisation, grounded in both economic rationale and governance stewardship.

Importantly, this is not about maximising extraction, it's about maximising alignment. Strategic monetisation must reward participation, enhance engagement, and enable the sustainability of the ecosystem itself.

At its core, this part answers a pivotal question: *How can associations monetise value without compromising trust, and turn contribution into both impact and income?*

Chapter 7. Revenue by Design: A Platform Monetisation Framework[6]

Beyond Dues and Events

In traditional associations, revenue was often seen as an outcome of member growth or program delivery. Dues were set annually, event tickets were priced per head, and sponsorship was packaged as exposure. These models worked, for a time, but they were never designed for the networked, digital, and expectation-rich environments associations now operate in.

As associations shift into platform-based models, monetisation cannot remain a bolt-on or legacy process. It must become a core design function. Revenue is no longer a question of pricing access to services. It is about how the association enables value, and how that value is ethically and sustainably shared between the organisation, its members, partners, and broader ecosystem actors.

This chapter builds on the principles introduced in *The Modern Association Playbook*, particularly the *Association Platform Success Framework* (APSF), and reframes monetisation as a strategic design challenge. It presents monetisation not as a financial lever, but as an economic outcome of interaction design, trust infrastructure, and network participation.

Key themes include:

- Aligning revenue models with business model archetypes and governance capacity
- Embedding ethical safeguards into data, pricing, and partnership strategies
- Mapping monetisation pathways across member and non-member actors
- Understanding when and how to commercialise participation, contribution, and insight
- Evaluating readiness for spin-outs, digital services, and ecosystem monetisation

Whether your association is seeking to stabilise income, diversify beyond dues, or fund a platform transformation, this chapter offers structured tools, strategic filters, and worked examples to guide the design of revenue models that reinforce mission and grow impact.

In the platform era, revenue does not follow from what you sell, it follows from how well you govern the value you enable.

---

[6] Because monetisation is the central component of strategic success it is covered in both *The Modern Association Playbook* and here.

Monetisation as a Design Function

In platform economics, revenue is not an afterthought. It is a design decision. Monetisation does not occur because an association happens to deliver something useful, it happens when the system of interactions is structured in a way that consistently produces value worth paying for.

Associations must move beyond the traditional question, *"How do we make money from what we do?", and ask,*

"How do we design interactions that are valuable enough to monetise, ethically, inclusively, and sustainably?"

This reframing is critical. It positions monetisation not as a separate commercial activity, but as a direct outcome of platform architecture. Every element of the system, from how participants contribute, how data is used, to how decisions are governed, influences whether people see enough value to pay, and whether that payment supports trust and long-term engagement.

Monetisation, in this model, becomes a function of:

- **Interaction design**, are we facilitating exchanges that matter to participants and solve meaningful problems?
- **Participation incentives**, are contributors motivated to create value that others are willing to pay for?
- **Trust and legitimacy**, are monetisation mechanisms aligned with the association's mission and member expectations?
- **Network dynamics**, does the system become more valuable as more people engage, and is that value distributed fairly?

This perspective requires associations to integrate economic thinking with governance design. It is not enough to price a product competitively. Associations must consider how pricing interacts with equity, access, data use, and stakeholder expectations. When these factors are misaligned, monetisation efforts risk backfiring, damaging trust or excluding key groups.

Successful monetisation in platform associations depends on:

- Structuring interactions that generate mutual value
- Identifying natural monetisation points within those interactions
- Embedding safeguards and governance mechanisms to ensure transparency and fairness
- Building flexibility into models so that they can adapt to changing participation patterns or ethical considerations

In short, monetisation is not just a financial tactic. It is a strategic design function that must be developed alongside value architecture, participation models, and governance structures.

Revenue Models in Practice: Menu of Strategic Options

Below is a categorised list of platform-era revenue options, many of which build directly on interaction design:

Table 7-1 Revenue Models

Model Type	Examples	Strategic Consideration
Subscription	Tiered memberships, CPD bundles	Must reflect segmented value, not just admin convenience
Transaction Fee	Marketplace cut, referral commissions	Works if platform matches buyers and sellers
Sponsorship	Digital placement, content integration, hosted events	Requires governance guardrails for ethical alignment
Freemium Access	Free base membership, paid for add-ons (e.g. analytics, advanced CPD)	Aligns well with younger members and experimentation
Data Services	Sector reports, benchmarking, industry dashboards	Must ensure trust, consent, and clear ethical frameworks
White-Labelling	Licensing platform tools or curriculum to others	Leverages sunk costs, expands reach
Spin-Out Ventures	Social enterprise arms, credentialing subsidiaries	Demands strong governance oversight and clarity of mission

Each revenue model must be assessed not only for viability, but for *strategic fit* with the association's role, trust position, and governance capacity.

Understanding Business Model Archetypes Before Monetising

Before designing new revenue streams, associations must first understand the economic engine they are operating. Monetisation is not a standalone act, it is the downstream expression of a business model. Without clarity on how value is created and exchanged, attempts to generate income risk being misaligned, ineffective, or even damaging to trust.

This section outlines four common business model archetypes in the association sector, and the implications of each for monetisation, engagement, and governance.

Table 7-2 Business Model Archetypes in the Association Landscape

Model Type	Value Logic	Monetisation Strategy	Risks / Considerations
Service Provider	Deliver defined programs to members	Fee-for-service, event income	Low scalability; easily commoditised
Subscription-Based	Membership bundles access to core services	Flat dues, limited tiers	Attrition risk if perceived value drops
Participation Platform	Enable value creation through interaction	Tiered services, data, sponsorship	High governance complexity, requires trust
Ecosystem Hub	Orchestrate multi-actor value at scale	Outcome-based, shared revenue, grants	Strategic alignment and ethical risk management

Choosing the Right Frame

Each model represents a different theory of value. A service-provider model assumes members are consumers. A subscription model assumes they value bundled access. A platform model assumes members want to participate, contribute, and co-create. An ecosystem model assumes value lies in network outcomes, not just transactions.

Before monetising, boards and executives should ask:

- *What kind of value do we enable, and for whom?*
- *Are we monetising access, interaction, or outcomes?*
- *Is our business model fit for the revenue models we are pursuing?*

Strategic Fit and Governance Implications

Monetisation without model alignment creates friction. For example:

- A platform-style monetisation approach (such as tiered CPD credits or data services) will struggle in a legacy service model where interaction isn't designed in.
- Ecosystem-level partnerships demand shared governance frameworks, not just contracts.
- Member contributions must be acknowledged and protected, otherwise monetisation can erode trust and participation.

The association's governance model must also evolve to match the business logic. Participation models require participatory governance. Ecosystem strategies demand adaptive oversight and cross-sector intelligence.

Tools to Support Business Model-Monetisation Fit

Several tools in this playbook and the companion *Economics of Modern Associations* can support this alignment:

- **Platform Revenue Model Matrix**: Maps revenue logic across direct vs indirect and association- vs member-generated value.
- **Monetisation Decision Matrix**: Evaluates ideas against criteria such as member impact, scalability, trust, and technical readiness.
- **ROPI (Return on Platform Investment) Framework**: Shifts financial analysis from traditional ROI to a platform-specific lens that captures alignment, engagement, and enablement outcomes.

Business models are not just about money, they are about meaning. They shape how members engage, how decisions are made, and how trust is earned. Getting the business model right is not a prerequisite to monetisation, it is its foundation.

The Platform Revenue Model Matrix

As platform associations evolve, monetisation must reflect how value is created, and who participates in that process. The ***Platform Revenue Model Matrix*** helps association leaders visualise and evaluate current and potential revenue streams across two key dimensions:

- Value origin: Who creates the value, the association, members, or external partners?
- Monetisation mode: Is revenue captured directly (via access or usage) or indirectly (via trust, data, or third-party relationships)?

This strategic tool allows associations to shift from transactional thinking to ecosystem-aware revenue design, enabling a more diverse and scalable portfolio.

Table 7-3 Platform Revenue Model Matrix

	Direct Monetisation (tied to access, usage, or service)	Indirect Monetisation (via data, trust, or adjacent services)
Value Created by Association	Paid CPD, publications, subscriptions *e.g. webinar fees, member portals*	Trust licensing, reputation-based partnerships *e.g. white-labelling, certification fees*
Value Created by Members	Peer marketplaces, mentoring fees *e.g. member-led CPD, paid contributions*	Sponsored communities, engagement analytics *e.g. insights from member forums*
Value Created by Partners / Ecosystem	Industry briefings, co-branded programs	Outcome payments, infrastructure grants

	e.g. sponsored webinars, partner CPD	*e.g. platform funding, policy impact projects*

Instructions for Use

1. Map current revenue streams.
2. Identify concentration risk or untapped areas.
3. Design a revenue mix that matches your governance capability and ecosystem role.

Strategic Insight

The matrix invites a powerful question:

If value is co-created,
how is that value shared, and
who governs the rules of exchange?

Governance and Monetisation Modes Matrix

To successfully operationalise new monetisation models, associations must ensure their governance systems are fit for purpose. The second matrix below maps three governance maturity levels against three types of monetisation logic, transactional, relational, and ecosystem-based.

This matrix helps boards evaluate whether they are structurally and culturally ready to support more advanced, participatory, or partnership-driven revenue models.

Table 7-4 Governance and Monetisation Modes Matrix

	Basic Governance	Strategic Governance	Participatory Governance
Transactional Monetisation: Fees for services, static pricing	Traditional event tickets, course fees, basic membership tiers	Modular CPD, tiered pricing, premium subscriptions	Limited applicability, participatory models require more flexible, reciprocal logic
Relational Monetisation: Value from member interaction, contributions	Difficult to govern, risks of burnout or inequality if unacknowledged	Member-led content, peer mentoring monetisation, contributor stipends	Community marketplaces, tokenised contribution models, co-created IP revenue sharing
Ecosystem Monetisation: Revenue from partnerships,	Grant funding, contracted services with minimal input from members	Co-branded partnerships, data dashboards, revenue-sharing MoUs	Platform licensing, shared ventures, data collaboratives with opt-in governance models

	Basic Governance	Strategic Governance	Participatory Governance
networks, data systems			

How to Use

- Use in strategic planning or governance reviews to assess readiness and misalignment risks.
- Layer this over the Platform Revenue Matrix to identify which models require stronger participatory oversight or ethical design frameworks.

Strategic Takeaway

Not all revenue models are governance-neutral. As associations explore peer-led services, data partnerships, or ecosystem monetisation, their governance structures must evolve, from centralised control to distributed trust stewardship.

Case Example: Designing Revenue into a Peer Mentoring Platform

The *Australasian Allied Health Association (AAHA)* operated a successful peer mentoring program to support early career practitioners. Initially volunteer-driven and funded through membership dues, the platform showed high engagement but growing strain on staff coordination, limited scalability, and no monetisation pathway.

Challenge:

The mentoring platform delivered real value, but it wasn't financially sustainable, nor was it clearly governed for future growth. Members asked for advanced features (analytics, scheduling tools, guided CPD links), but budgets were flat. The board faced a question: *Could we monetise this interaction without undermining trust or participation?*

Solution: Monetisation as Design, Not Extraction

Instead of bolting on a fee, AAHA applied the Platform Revenue Model Matrix and Governance and Monetisation Modes Matrix introduced earlier:

Interaction Design: They segmented mentoring into three tiers:

- **Tier 1 (Open):** Basic matching and resource access (free, member benefit)
- **Tier 2 (Enhanced):** Scheduling tools, peer feedback summaries, CPD tracking ($49 annual add-on)
- **Tier 3 (Certified Mentor Pathway):** Structured contribution hours, formal recognition, and exclusive webinars ($149/year)

Participation Incentives:

- Certified mentors could access CPD credits and gain preferred status in speaker panels.
- High contributors were eligible for paid content partnerships and were showcased at the annual summit.

Ethical Governance:

- An Ethics and Participation Committee was formed to oversee value exchange and evaluate fairness.
- Non-monetised pathways remained available to ensure inclusion.
- Feedback loops were embedded (NPS, contribution surveys, opt-outs) to prevent mission drift.

Results:

- Within 12 months, they expected to have over 20 percent of users upgraded to Tier 2 or 3.
- Annual revenue from mentoring monetisation to exceed $75,000 with a > 92 percent satisfaction rate.
- Mentors reported higher satisfaction, citing increased visibility and tangible recognition.
- Sponsors began underwriting targeted mentor pathways linked to workforce development.

The AAHA's monetisation strategy succeeded because it treated revenue as the outcome of interaction design, governance trust, and strategic framing, not as a simple charge for access. It preserved equity, enhanced engagement, and created new value streams without undermining the platform's legitimacy.

Calculations:

To generate $75,000 in annual revenue from the tiered mentoring model, the Australasian Allied Health Association (AAHA) would need approximately 5,068 total users on the platform.

Financial Breakdown:

20 percent of users upgrade to a paid tier → about 1,014 paying users

Tier 2 ($49/year): ~760 users (75 percent of payers) → $37,240

Tier 3 ($149/year): ~254 users (25 percent of payers) → $37,846

Total revenue: $75,086

Assumptions

75:25 split between Tier 2 and Tier 3 adopters among paying users

No sponsor income included in this base model

Revenue comes entirely from member upgrades

Ethical Monetisation and the Role of Governance

Monetisation is not morally neutral. In associations, revenue generation is entangled with trust, and members expect that financial decisions will align with the organisation's mission, values, and public purpose. A poorly designed revenue model can erode legitimacy faster than it raises funds.

Boards must therefore adopt a *dual lens* when evaluating new monetisation strategies:

1. **Revenue Sustainability:** Is this model financially viable, scalable, and aligned with our long-term economic capacity?
2. **Ethical Legitimacy:** Does this model reinforce, rather than undermine, our social contract with members, contributors, and external stakeholders?

This is where governance becomes central. It is not sufficient to run a profitability analysis. Associations must evaluate the distributional effects, power dynamics, and trust impacts of their monetisation decisions.

The role of the Company Secretary and governance professionals is critical. Their responsibility extends beyond procedural compliance. It includes:

- Ensuring that monetisation proposals are subject to ethical oversight and stakeholder consultation
- Embedding values-based criteria into commercial assessments, such as reciprocity, equity, and transparency
- Supporting the board to implement fit-for-purpose governance mechanisms, such as data ethics charters, sponsor codes, or conflict-of-interest frameworks, that enable revenue generation without compromising trust

In a platform context, governance is not a brake on monetisation. It is the scaffolding that allows it to scale without fracturing the institution's core purpose.

Commercialisation Readiness

Not all associations are immediately equipped to pursue diversified or platform-based revenue models. Effective monetisation requires more than opportunity identification, it demands clarity of purpose, governance maturity, and organisational adaptability.

To support structured assessment, the *Commercialisation Readiness Scorecard* provides a practical diagnostic for boards and executive teams. It identifies the core capabilities and conditions required to pursue new revenue streams ethically, sustainably, and strategically.

Table 7-5 Commercialisation Readiness Scorecard

Dimension	High Readiness Indicator
Strategic Clarity	Clear, shared articulation of the value proposition across target segments
Data Capability	Reliable analytics on member behaviour, service usage, and participation
Governance Alignment	Delegations, controls, and oversight frameworks in place for new initiatives
Cultural Readiness	Board and staff exhibit openness to experimentation and iterative design
Risk Appetite	Risk profile is defined, debated, and actively governed at board level

This tool is best used during strategic planning, budget formulation, or business model review processes. It helps ensure that commercial decisions are grounded in both institutional self-awareness and practical feasibility, reducing the risk of overreach or reputational strain.

A low score in any one dimension does not mean monetisation is off the table. It signals where investment, dialogue, or capability-building is needed before proceeding.

Australian Case Examples

Smart Precinct NQ

An innovation hub that blends place-based entrepreneurship with community engagement. Revenue sources include sponsored events, innovation grants, co-working subscriptions, and a partnership monetisation strategy. Governance oversight ensures alignment between local development goals and platform logic.

Guild Insurance & APS

The Australian Psychological Society offers member insurance via Guild, with negotiated pricing and tailored features. While indirect, this monetised partnership demonstrates ecosystem orchestration, not just service provision.

Key Considerations for Strategic Monetisation

- **Start with value, not revenue**: Monetisation works best when it follows proven demand.
- **Model scenarios**: Test different pricing models, segment strategies, and ecosystem offers.
- **Design for iteration**: Early pilots, limited releases, and feedback loops reduce risk.
- **Maintain mission clarity**: Revenue should reinforce, not replace, purpose.

Orchestrating Sustainable Revenue

Revenue, in a platform-based association, is not just about financial survival. It is about enabling deeper engagement, broader impact, and extended reach. When monetisation is designed with care, governed with integrity, and aligned to real value flows, it becomes a strategic capability, not a distraction.

This chapter has repositioned revenue generation as a design function. It has introduced tools, models, and strategic filters to support associations in building monetisation strategies that reflect their mission, respect member trust, and unlock new value across the ecosystem.

In the next chapter, we turn to pricing, unpacking the practical and ethical considerations of setting, communicating, and evolving value-based pricing strategies for platform participation.

[illegible]

Australian Case Examples

[illegible]

Key Considerations for [illegible] Monetisation

- [illegible]
- [illegible]
- [illegible]
- [illegible]

Orchestrating [illegible] Revenue

[illegible]

Summary: Revenue by Design, A Platform Monetisation Framework

1. Monetisation Is a Design Function, Not Just a Financial Target

Revenue in platform associations must emerge from value flows, not administrative convenience. It should be designed into user interactions, ecosystem logic, and participation incentives.

2. The Platform Revenue Matrix Unlocks New Revenue Paths

Associations can monetise across four key domains:

- Association-created products and services (dues, learning)
- Association-leveraged influence (grants, sponsorships)
- User-driven contributions (job boards, peer consulting)
- Third-party engagement with users (advertisers, funders)

3. Ethical Monetisation Requires Governance Stewardship

Boards must balance sustainability with legitimacy. Revenue must align with member trust, purpose, and the social contract of the association. Mission clarity is non-negotiable.

4. New Models Require Commercialisation Readiness

Before diversification, assess governance controls, data capacity, cultural appetite, and risk alignment. A Commercialisation Readiness Scorecard supports disciplined expansion.

5. Revenue Models Must Evolve with the Ecosystem

Freemium tiers, data services, platform licensing, and spin-outs all represent future-ready approaches, but only when trust infrastructure, feedback loops, and ethical safeguards are in place.

Chapter 8. Platform Economics Formulas

This chapter is a brief introduction to the maths to enable measurement of the attributes that make platforms so powerful. A more detailed account is contained in Part VI.

This chapter brings together the key formulas and conceptual tools introduced throughout the book in a single, structured location. Readers seeking technical depth or applying platform logic to pricing, engagement, or design decisions can refer to this section, while core chapters remain focused on strategic narrative and use cases.

Pricing and Participation Optimisation

Total Platform Value

The optimal price structure maximises total platform value (Vp) -

$$Vp = \sum_{i=0}^{n} PiQi - C$$

Where:

Pi Price charged to group i (e.g., users or providers).

Qi Quantity of group i participants.

C Total operating cost of the platform.

Cross-Side Network Effects

Effect of Growth on Opposing Platform Side

Multi-sided platforms thrive on cross-side interdependence. An increase in users on one side often boosts the utility and growth of the other. This is captured by:

$$Nij = \frac{\partial Qi}{\partial Qj}$$

Where:

Nij represents how an increase in participants on one side (Qj) affects participation on the other side (Qi).

Nij Cross-side network effect between group i and j.

Ui Utility of participants on side i. (See below)

Qj Quantity of participants on side j.

If $Nij>0$, there is a positive cross-side effect; if $Nij<0$, there is a negative cross-side effect.

→ *See Chapter 16.4 for pricing strategy implications*

Match Quality and Utility Metrics

Match Quality Score (Relevance-Weighted Engagement)

A. Relevance Score (R)

$$\overline{R} = \frac{1}{n}\sum_{i=1}^{n} R_i$$

R_i: User-rated relevance (e.g. 1–5 stars)
n: Number of completed feedback responses
→ Helps refine search filters, recommendation engines, and segmentation logic.

B. Interaction Density (Ecosystem Stickiness)

$$ID = \frac{T}{U_a}$$

T: Total interactions (e.g. messages, course starts, forum replies)
U_a: Active users during the period
→ **Higher ID** suggests a "sticky" platform where users actively participate.

Cost Efficiency and Scaling

C. Cost Per User

Platforms aggregate costs across participants to generate economies of scale. The cost per user, Cu, decreases as the number of users increases -

$$Cu = \frac{Cf}{Qt} + Cv$$

Where:

Cf - Fixed costs (e.g., IT infrastructure).

Qt - Total number of participants on the platform.

Cv - Variable costs per user (e.g., customer support).

As Qt grows, Cu approaches Cv, driving cost efficiencies and increasing profitability.

Use in: Chapter 16 *(Cost Models)*

Return on Platform Investment (ROPI)

D. Platform-Focused ROI Measure

$$ROPI = \frac{Net\ Benefits\ (Gains - Costs)}{Total\ Costs}\ x\ 100$$

ROPI adapts traditional ROI logic to platform dynamics by capturing intangible value flows (e.g. trust, engagement, shared IP).

Chapter 9. Pricing, Packaging, and Member-Centred Strategy

From Cost Recovery to Value Recognition

In legacy association models, pricing was largely administrative. Dues were set to cover operating costs, event fees matched venue and catering expenses, and publications were priced per unit or bundled into membership. The logic was transactional, built around cost recovery.

Platform-based associations operate in a different economic context, one shaped by network effects, variable contributions, diverse participant roles, and differentiated value creation. In this environment, pricing is no longer just a financial mechanism. It is a strategic lever that influences participation, signals value, and structures how members, partners, and contributors interact with the platform.

Pricing now sits at the intersection of economics, ethics, and engagement. It raises questions not only about affordability, but about fairness, recognition, and trust.

This chapter reframes pricing as a platform coordination tool, rather than a revenue tactic. It explores how associations can design pricing models that:

- Reflect value, not just cost
- Recognise contribution and participation
- Support inclusion without undermining sustainability
- Align with member outcomes and mission impact

The goal is not simply to price services more effectively, but to design pricing systems that reinforce the economic and social logic of the platform.

When Tiered Pricing Failed, Then Succeeded

The Australian Learning & Development Association (ALDA) had long used a flat-fee membership model: $220 per year, regardless of role, engagement, or value received. While administratively simple, the model began to show cracks. Senior professionals felt they were subsidising early-career members, while newer entrants questioned the cost relative to free content available elsewhere.

In 2022, ALDA introduced a three-tiered model:

- Core ($99): Basic access to events and news
- Professional ($249): Added CPD, toolkits, and job board access
- Premier ($599): Executive roundtables, custom insights, and advisory access

Uptake was modest. But dissatisfaction grew. Members felt uncertain about the value at each tier. Some Premier-tier members discovered they were paying more for features they didn't use. Others didn't upgrade because they weren't sure what was behind the paywall. A year later, retention dipped.

Rather than abandon the tiers, ALDA restructured its pricing using *value-based principles:*

Member contribution data was used to personalise access levels

Toolkits and CPD were packaged based on actual usage patterns

A clear "value map" showed what was included, why it mattered, and who benefited

Feedback loops allowed members to adjust their tier quarterly

The results: Premier renewals jumped significantly. Per-member revenue rose. And trust in the new model increased, not because it was cheaper, but because it made sense.

Strategic Insight

Pricing is not about charging more. It's about showing members how their participation, contribution, and career journey connect to tangible, differentiated value, and giving them options that reflect that.

When Value-Based Pricing Backfired

The National Association of Health Communicators (NAHC) wanted to modernise its pricing model. Inspired by platform economics, the board approved a shift from flat annual dues to a dynamic, engagement-weighted pricing structure. Members who used more services or accessed premium tools would pay more; those who contributed to the community (e.g. via mentoring or speaking) would receive discounts.

The intention was to reward participation and align revenue with member value. But there was a problem:

- NAHC lacked the infrastructure, trust, and communication capability to support the transition.
- The algorithm behind pricing changes was not explained clearly
- Contribution metrics were inconsistently recorded
- Members received confusing invoices with variable pricing each quarter
- Some long-time members felt penalised for using the services they had helped build

Social media backlash followed. A group of members described the model as "*gamified compliance*." Within six months, the board paused the initiative and reverted to the old pricing structure, issuing credits and apologies.

Strategic Insight

Value-based pricing is only effective when backed by transparent data, clear communication, and established trust. Without these foundations, even well-intentioned models can appear arbitrary or extractive, undermining the very engagement they are meant to incentivise.

Table 9-1 Transitioning to Value-Based Pricing, Lessons from the Field

Case	What Worked or Did Not	Key Insight
ALDA – Tiered Pricing Reworked	What worked: refined tiers using real usage data; communicated a clear value map; enabled flexible movement between tiers	Pricing success depends on aligning cost with perceived and actual value, not just role or seniority
NAHC – Dynamic Pricing Backfired	What did not work: rolled out without member consultation; poor communication of the logic; no governance for exceptions or appeal	Even a sound model will fail if trust, transparency, and infrastructure are missing

Table 9-2 Practical Guidance: Designing Member-Centred Pricing

Recommended Practice	Common Pitfall to Avoid
Involve members early in co-design and testing	Introduce pricing changes without a clear or shared rationale
Use real data to segment by value and contribution	Assume role or job title equals value perception
Create flexibility for members to self-select and upgrade tiers	Lock members into rigid pricing levels that do not reflect changing needs
Communicate how pricing supports fairness, inclusion, and mission	Obscure pricing logic behind unclear systems or automated changes
Build in a regular review and feedback loop	Treat pricing as a one-time decision without adapting to member response

Pricing as a Strategic Lever

Pricing does more than generate revenue. It is one of the most powerful design tools available to associations. It signals value, shapes behaviour, and structures participation. In a platform-based model, where members are contributors as well as consumers, pricing becomes part of the association's economic architecture, not just its financial plan.

There are three core strategic functions of pricing:

- **Signal**: Pricing reflects the perceived value of what is offered. A higher price can signal exclusivity, depth, or strategic importance (e.g. premium analytics or executive roundtables).
- **Filter**: Pricing acts as a gatekeeper, influencing who participates and at what level. It can ensure commitment, prioritise serious users, or protect capacity in limited-access environments.

- **Incentive**: Pricing can shape desired behaviours, such as offering discounts for contributors, loyalty rewards, or early access pricing to encourage timely action.

These functions must be consciously designed. Pricing should align with the association's purpose, platform logic, and participation goals. Relying on legacy fee structures risks sending the wrong signals, creating unintentional barriers, or distorting engagement patterns.

Strategic pricing begins with one core question: *What behaviours and value relationships are we trying to enable, and what pricing logic supports them?*

Why Legacy Pricing Models Fail

Many associations carry hidden distortions in their pricing structures, legacies of older models that no longer reflect how value is created, delivered, or experienced. These distortions are not just financial issues. They shape member behaviour, erode trust, and constrain strategic flexibility.

Common examples include:

- **Over-subsidising high-value segments:** High-engagement members who contribute content, mentor peers, or lead initiatives often pay the same as passive members, despite generating far greater value for the community.
- **Flat pricing models :** Uniform fees disregard differences in capacity to pay or in value received, discouraging both entry-level participation and deeper investment from those willing to engage more fully.
- **Undercharging for ecosystem services:** Activities such as matchmaking, benchmarking, or knowledge curation are labour-intensive and strategically important, yet they are often unmonetised or buried within general dues.
- **Overreliance on external sponsorship:** When member pricing fails to cover the cost of value creation, associations often turn to sponsors, sometimes compromising independence or over-commercialising community spaces.

These issues reflect a broader challenge: a disconnect between economic design and engagement realities. In a platform-based association, pricing must reflect the actual contribution, usage, and perceived value experienced by diverse participant groups.

Correcting mispricing is not just about charging more. It is about aligning the revenue model with the lived economics of participation.

Reframing Value: Principles of Strategic Pricing

Value-based pricing shifts the focus from what a product or service costs to produce, to what it is worth to the user. In a platform-based association, where value is often co-created and influenced by context, this approach provides a more flexible, equitable, and strategically aligned method of setting prices.

Value is shaped by multiple factors:

- **Usefulness:** What outcomes does this offering help a member achieve? Does it save time, solve a problem, build influence, or accelerate learning?
- **Comparables:** What would members pay for equivalent experiences or services elsewhere? How does the association's offering compare in quality, credibility, and convenience?
- **Network Effects:** How much additional value is created when others participate? For example, peer forums, mentoring schemes, or job boards grow more useful as participation increases.
- **Mission Fit:** What price point supports both sustainability and access? Does the pricing structure reinforce the association's commitment to inclusion, fairness, and long-term engagement?

Illustrative contrast:

A leadership roundtable may be inexpensive to deliver but offers high strategic value to a senior executive. It may justify a premium fee due to exclusivity, insight, and peer exposure.

By contrast, baseline access to community discussion forums might be priced low, or provided free, to maximise engagement, inclusivity, and the broader benefits of a vibrant network.

Effective value-based pricing ensures that members are not paying for content alone, but for outcomes, credibility, and connection.

Worked Example: Applying Value-Based Pricing in a Professional Association

Scenario: The Association of Digital Health Professionals (ADHP) offers three services:

Baseline Community Access: Includes discussion forums, digital bulletin, and peer Q&A.

Advanced Career Accelerator Program: A six-month mentored cohort with exclusive industry speakers.

AI Literacy for Health Leaders: A micro credentialed course co-developed with a university partner.

Traditional Pricing Approach: All three services were previously bundled into a standard $275 membership, with little transparency on how the pricing related to usage or value.

Table 9-3 Value-Based Redesign

Offering	Usefulness	Comparables	Network Effects	Mission Fit	New Pricing Strategy
Community Access	Medium – everyday utility, networking	Free LinkedIn groups, but lower relevance	High – more users improves experience	High – aligns with inclusion goals	Free for all members (baseline tier), sponsored via partner support
Career Accelerator	High – targeted outcomes, executive visibility	$2,000 to $3,000 for similar private programs	Medium – small cohort benefits from selectivity	Medium – not for all members	$950 program fee, with partial scholarships offered
AI Literacy Course	High – sector relevance and credentials	$400 to $600 in university MOOCs	Low – individualised	High – builds system capacity	$295 course fee, bundled at discount for Professional-tier members

Result:

- Participation in the community forum increased 48%
- Accelerator filled in under two weeks, with 15% of seats via equity scholarship
- Course uptake exceeded forecast by 22%, supported by bundled pricing

Strategic Insight

Value-based pricing enabled differentiation, supported access, and improved both revenue and impact, without commoditising core services.

Tool: Value-Based Pricing Decision Canvas

Use this canvas in product or pricing reviews to map how an offering aligns with core pricing principles:

Table 9-4 Pricing Canvas

Dimension	Strategic Question	Your Answer / Notes
Usefulness	What outcomes does this service deliver for members?	
Comparables	What would members pay for a similar product or service externally?	

Dimension	Strategic Question	Your Answer / Notes
Network Effects	Does this service become more valuable as more members use it?	
Mission Fit	How does this pricing model support fairness, equity, and long-term engagement?	
Revenue Alignment	Is the pricing sufficient to support sustainable delivery, development, and governance of this service?	
Participation Model	Should this be priced individually, bundled, or used to incentivise deeper engagement?	

How to Use:

- Use during program design, pricing reviews, or budget planning.
- Consider involving member advisory groups to test assumptions.
- Review quarterly or annually as part of strategy refresh.

Having established the principles of value-based pricing, we now turn to participation-aligned models that translate those principles into flexible pricing structures.

Models of Participation-Centred Pricing

Platform associations operate in environments where engagement is dynamic, contribution is variable, and member expectations differ by role, region, and stage of career. This demands pricing models that reflect participation patterns, not just access rights.

Table 9-5 Participation-Centred Pricing

Model Type	Description	Use Case
Tiered Access	Members choose from levels of benefit	Differentiated CPD, analytics, networking
Freemium to Premium	Base access is free; advanced tools are paid	Data dashboards, career coaching
Pay-per-use	No fixed fee; price per event/service	Webinar passes, mentoring sessions
Contribution Credits	Discounts earned through volunteering, sharing	Event passes, CPD credits
Dynamic Pricing	Prices shift by timing, volume, or demand	Early bird rates, limited-edition offers
Equity Pricing	Lower fees for students, regionals, low income	Inclusive access without structural loss

Each model offers a distinct way to balance participation, value, and sustainability. However, successful implementation requires attention to:

- **Simplicity of communication:** Members must understand the structure quickly and clearly.
- **Alignment with platform design:** Pricing should reinforce participation pathways, not disrupt them.
- **Governance and compliance:** Especially important for models involving volunteering, peer ratings, or reward schemes, where transparency and fairness must be safeguarded.

Packaging for Perceived and Strategic Value

Pricing rarely stands alone. The way value is *packaged,* framed, grouped, and communicated, strongly influences how members perceive worth and make decisions.

In a crowded environment, smart packaging can reduce cognitive load, improve conversion, and align offers with member journeys.

Best Practice Packaging Techniques

- **Outcome framing:** Emphasise the *result* rather than the format. For example, "*Advance your career*" is more compelling than "*Webinar bundle.*"
- **Thematic offers:** Group offerings around member journeys, such as "*Early-Career Accelerator*" or "*Leadership Growth Pathway,*" rather than by department or format.
- **Cross-partner bundles:** Include access to other organisations' products or services. For example, joint CPD credentials, co-hosted masterclasses, or partner-led diagnostics.
- **Scaffolded tiers:** Build a progression ladder from low-commitment, low-cost offerings to premium, high-investment services, allowing members to grow with the platform.

When thoughtfully designed, packaging increases perceived value, supports uptake, and provides members with clearer choices that align with their needs and ambitions.

Table 9-6 Pricing-Packaging Map

Tier / Offer Type	Price Strategy	Key Features	Value Proposition
Free / Baseline Access	Freemium / Sponsored	Forum access, updates, event previews	Stay connected and informed
Starter / Student	Equity Pricing	Discounted CPD, career tools, curated resources	Build your foundation
Professional Tier	Tiered Subscription	Full CPD, dashboards, job board	Advance your skills and career
Premier Tier	Premium / High-Touch	Strategic roundtables, insights, analytics	Lead and influence your profession
Pay-per-use	Transactional / Flexible	Individual webinars, mentoring, short courses	Access what you need, when you need it
Contributor Tier	Earned Credit / Discount	Volunteer rewards, peer recognition	Give back and gain access
Partner Bundle	Co-branded / Licensed	Access to joint content, tools, and services	Broaden your impact across the sector

Ethical Considerations in Pricing

As not-for-profit and public-purpose institutions, associations have an obligation to price with purpose. Revenue must not come at the expense of trust, equity, or legitimacy. In a platform environment, where pricing can signal status, shape participation, and influence power dynamics, ethics must be built into every monetisation decision.

Ethical Pricing Principles:

- Avoid exploitative upselling: Members should never feel pressured into unnecessary upgrades or paywalls that restrict core professional participation.
- Ensure transparency: Clear communication about what is free, subsidised, or premium avoids confusion and reinforces trust.
- Protect public interest: Pricing structures must avoid perceptions of policy capture, such as sponsor-exclusive access to regulatory or advocacy spaces.
- Uphold equity: Particularly in health, education, and profession-adjacent sectors, pricing should reflect capacity to pay and ensure inclusive access to services.

Mini Case Lens: The Role of Governance in Pricing Decisions

When the Board of the National Allied Professionals Association introduced a multi-tier pricing structure for professional development access, the initiative was intended to increase uptake among younger members while creating new revenue pathways. However, concerns soon emerged about perceived inequities in access. A review panel chaired by the Company Secretary identified the absence of an ethical pricing framework and inconsistent approval pathways for price changes.

In response, the Board implemented a Pricing Ethics Policy, established a delegated approval schedule, and required all significant pricing changes to undergo review by the Risk and Governance Committee. The Company Secretary led the development of pricing impact disclosures, published quarterly to ensure transparency and strengthen internal trust.

This example illustrates why pricing must be treated not only as a financial lever but as a governance responsibility.

Governance Role: Boards and governance professionals must actively oversee pricing frameworks that affect:

- Access to core services or benefits
- Member inclusion and diversity
- Public reputation and trust
- Strategic alignment with purpose and mission

The Company Secretary plays a critical enabling role, ensuring pricing decisions are risk-aware, policy-aligned, and member-legitimate. Ethical monetisation requires clear documentation, member-centred review processes, and board-level safeguards to ensure pricing enhances rather than erodes public value.

Practical Framework: Designing a Pricing Strategy

A practical approach to redesigning pricing and packaging might include:

- **Segment Mapping** – Understand user archetypes and their value perceptions
- **Contribution Analysis** – Assess who is creating vs consuming value
- **Willingness-to-Pay Estimation** – Use surveys, test pricing, pilot models
- **Model Simulation** – Forecast financial and engagement impacts
- **Board Oversight** – Ensure policy, ethics, and risk alignment
- **Iterate and Review** – Treat pricing as a dynamic strategy, not a fixed decision

Practical Framework: Designing a Pricing Strategy

A Six-Step Approach to Align Price with Value, Participation, and Purpose

1. Segment Mapping

Goal: Understand who your users are, what they value, and how they engage.

Tool: *Member Persona Map*
Map key user types across these dimensions:

- Motivation (e.g. learning, networking, influence)
- Value perception (e.g. convenience, prestige, social impact)
- Engagement pattern (e.g. episodic, intensive, peripheral)
- Price sensitivity (e.g. cost-conscious, value-first)

Outcome: Enables differentiated pricing and packaging that reflects member journeys.

2. Contribution Analysis

Goal: Identify which users create value, which consume it, and where imbalances exist.

Tool: *Contribution–Incentive Matrix* (from Chapter 5)

Evaluate:

- Time-based contributions (volunteering, mentoring)
- Data and content contributions (forums, resources)
- Financial contributions (dues, purchases, sponsorship)

Outcome: Supports fairer, more strategic alignment of pricing with engagement effort.

3. Willingness-to-Pay Estimation

Goal: Understand how different user segments perceive value and what they are prepared to pay.

Tools:

- *Surveys* with value-ranking questions and price brackets
- *A/B pricing tests* for events or new digital services
- *Early access pilots* to trial premium tiers or bundles

Outcome: Sets evidence-based pricing floors and ceilings for packages and services.

4. Model Simulation

Goal: Forecast the financial, behavioural, and trust implications of different pricing scenarios.

Tools:

- *Scenario Planning Grid* - Compare low/medium/high uptake across models (e.g. freemium, tiered, usage-based).

- *Sensitivity Analysis* - Test what happens if 10% of high contributors disengage vs. 20% of low-value users upgrade.

Outcome: Informs risk-managed decisions grounded in both mission and margin.

5. Board Oversight and Policy Alignment

Goal: Ensure pricing strategy upholds the association's mission, equity principles, and risk appetite.

Tools:

- Ethical Pricing Checklist
    - ✅ Transparent?
    - ✅ Equitable?
    - ✅ Mission-aligned?
    - ✅ Sponsor-proofed?
- *Delegations of Authority Map* - Clarifies what levels of pricing change require board, CEO, or committee approval.

Outcome: Strengthens trust and accountability while allowing strategic flexibility.

6. Iterate and Review

Goal: Treat pricing as a dynamic, evolving part of strategy, not a once-set policy.

Tools:

- *Post-launch dashboards* (retention, conversion, satisfaction by tier)
- *User interviews* (especially non-renewers and downgraders)
- *Annual pricing review cycle* linked to strategic plan refresh

Outcome: Builds internal agility and long-term pricing resilience.

Case Insight: OpenLearning (AU)

Platform: OpenLearning offers a modular social learning platform used by universities, education providers, and learners globally.

Pricing Design Elements:

Freemium core: Basic platform usage is free, removing barriers to entry.

Premium tools: Paid tiers offer credentialing, analytics, and advanced content delivery.

Segment alignment: Educators pay based on usage and feature access; learners pay for certified pathways.

Incentive design: Features promote ongoing contribution (e.g. discussion engagement = better course performance).

Lessons for Associations:

✅ Clear segmentation supports scalable pricing

✅ Usage-linked models align cost with actual value creation

✅ Ongoing engagement is rewarded, not just initial payment

✅ Transparency builds trust in what is paid, free, or sponsored

Price is Strategy

In platform-based associations, pricing is not simply a financial task. It is a strategic design choice that shapes how value is experienced, how trust is built, and how participation is scaled.

When designed well, pricing:

- Signals value and sets expectations
- Filters and guides participation
- Rewards contribution and supports inclusion
- Aligns revenue with mission, not just market demand

The core challenge is not just to "get the price right" in a technical sense, but to get the logic right, ensuring the pricing approach reflects the real dynamics of modern member ecosystems. That means thinking beyond cost recovery or flat fees and embracing models that reinforce equity, engagement, and platform growth.

In the next chapter, we shift from pricing to evaluation: how associations can measure the true return on their platform investments using the ROPI (Return on Platform Investment) framework, and how these insights can inform strategy, governance, and member value creation.

Summary: Pricing, Packaging, and Member-Centred Strategy

1. Pricing Is Not Neutral, It's Strategic Design

In a platform association, pricing shapes behaviour, signals value, filters access, and defines incentive logic. It is no longer just about cost recovery, it's about designing participation and sustaining trust.

2. Mispricing Undermines Engagement and Equity

Flat dues, over-subsidised high-value users, and underpriced ecosystem services distort participation. Misalignment between contribution and pricing weakens both engagement and revenue integrity.

3. Value-Based Pricing Reflects Outcomes, Not Inputs

Effective pricing accounts for usefulness, comparables, network effects, and mission alignment. What something *costs to produce* matters less than what it's *worth to the user*, and to the ecosystem.

4. Participation-Centred Models Unlock Flexibility

Tiered access, contribution credits, dynamic pricing, and freemium models better reflect modern engagement patterns. They reward activity, encourage discovery, and balance inclusivity with sustainability.

5. Packaging Is the Communication Layer of Pricing

How value is bundled, named, and offered influences uptake. Outcome framing, themed journeys, and cross-partner offers help members understand not just what they get, but *why it matters*.

6. Ethics and Governance Are Non-Negotiable

Associations must price with integrity. That means transparent tiering, equity safeguards, and board oversight of pricing models that impact access, mission delivery, or public trust.

7. Pricing Strategy Must Be Iterative and Informed

Segmentation, contribution analysis, willingness-to-pay testing, and financial simulation form the foundation of strategic pricing. Governance and member insight complete the loop.

Chapter 10. Return on Platform Investment (ROPI)

The Investment Logic Behind the Platform

In the traditional association world, return on investment (ROI) was a relatively simple equation: if the revenue from a program exceeded its cost, it was deemed successful. But this approach is inadequate for platform-based associations, where value creation is distributed, intangible, and cumulative.

What's needed is a new lens, *Return on Platform Investment (ROPI)*, that captures the systemic, multi-actor, and time-dependent returns generated by platform-based strategies.

This chapter introduces the concept of ROPI, explains why traditional ROI fails in a platform context, and provides tools for association leaders to assess, track, and communicate the full value of their platform investments.

Why Traditional ROI Falls Short

Traditional ROI models focus on direct, linear returns:

"*We spent $X on a new website. Did we generate $Y in new revenue?*"

But platform-based investments often:

- Deliver *indirect* value (e.g. increased engagement, trust, network density)
- Have *delayed payoffs* (e.g. member-led communities that take time to grow)
- Produce *multi-sided value* (e.g. job boards benefiting members, partners, and employers)
- Require *shared infrastructure* (e.g. credentialing systems used by multiple stakeholders)

A more sophisticated model is required, one that reflects these features without reducing them to shallow proxies.

Defining ROPI: Return on Platform Investment

ROPI is a strategic evaluation model designed for platform-based associations. It considers:

- Ecosystem-wide value: How many actors benefit and how?
- Engagement amplification: Are interactions becoming more frequent or meaningful?
- Infrastructure leverage: Are core investments (e.g. CRM, content platform) supporting multiple outcomes?
- Strategic alignment: Does the investment reinforce mission, trust, and future positioning?

The key shift is from program ROI to platform performance.

ROPI Framework: Core Components

ROPI can be structured into five dimensions:

Table 10-1 Return on Platform Investment

Dimension	Description	Indicators
Reach	Growth in participation, stakeholders, and access	User numbers, diversity, geographic spread
Engagement	Depth, frequency, and quality of interaction	Active use metrics, repeat visits, contributions
Value Exchange	Number and quality of transactions enabled	Jobs posted, content shared, referrals
Platform Leverage	Efficiency and reuse of core infrastructure or content	Multi-program use of CRM, shared data assets
Strategic Alignment	Advancement of mission, trust, and long-term positioning	Surveyed trust, reputational indicators, ESG fit

Each of these dimensions can be tracked via metrics, stories, and investment reviews.

Calculating and Visualising ROPI

While ROPI is not reducible to a single number, a dashboard approach allows leadership teams to track progress:

Table 10-2 ROPI Dashboard

Metric	Target	Actual	Trend
Active Monthly Users	5,000	4,200	↑
Repeat Engagement Rate	40%	37%	→
Cross-Program Platform Use	6 units	8	↑
Data Value Redeployed (times)	10x	6x	→
Stakeholder Trust Index	80%	82%	↑

Such a dashboard combines quantitative insight with qualitative framing, making it suitable for board reporting and strategic review.

Applying ROPI to Strategic Investments

ROPI is especially useful for evaluating:

- CRM/AMS modernisation: Are data flows improving insight across multiple programs?

- Community platforms: Are contributions rising and peer value being generated?
- Credentialing systems: Are multiple partners adopting and co-owning standards?
- Open learning initiatives: Are partners, members, and non-members gaining value?

Boards can use ROPI to justify reinvestment, evaluate pilots, and defend infrastructure upgrades that may not show short-term financial ROI but deliver platform capacity.

ROPI and Risk: Investing in Strategic Optionality

Traditional risk frameworks often emphasise mitigation, the containment of downside exposure through controls and compliance. But in platform-based associations, a more adaptive risk posture is required, one that also accounts for *upside risk*, or the capacity to pivot, absorb disruption, and unlock emergent value.

This is where **Return on Platform Investment (ROPI)** adds strategic depth to risk management.

Optionality as a Proxy for Resilience

Optionality refers to the *latent capacity* of a platform to serve unanticipated future purposes. In a volatile environment, optionality is not a luxury, it is a form of preparedness. Associations with well-designed platforms can respond to crises, shifts in policy, or member needs with speed and credibility.

Examples of platform-enabled optionality:

- A community portal that can pivot into a crisis response centre during emergencies.
- A micro-credentialing system that becomes a national standard via external recognition.
- An open API infrastructure that enables new commercial or public-good partnerships.

Where traditional ROI struggles to justify such investments (due to delayed or indirect returns), ROPI reframes them as strategic assets, part of the organisation's adaptive capacity.

Integrating ROPI into Risk Governance

Boards and risk committees should begin to treat ROPI indicators as forward-looking *resilience signals*. For example:

Table 10-3 ROPI: Risk

ROPI Dimension	Related Risk Consideration
Engagement	Risk of disengagement, declining trust, or platform fatigue
Platform Leverage	Risk of duplicated infrastructure, sunk costs, or underuse
Strategic Alignment	Risk of drift from mission, member alienation, or ethical failure
Value Exchange	Risk of platform stagnation, free-riding, or equity failures
Optionality (new lens)	Risk of strategic rigidity, inability to adapt or partner

By embedding ROPI into enterprise risk management, associations can shift from managing threats to *governing resilience*. The ability to measure, justify, and steward platform investments becomes a strategic risk response in itself.

Governance Action:

- Integrate ROPI indicators into quarterly board dashboards alongside financial and risk reports.
- Use the ROPI Canvas (Section 8.8) in risk reviews to test long-term flexibility, stakeholder alignment, and infrastructure interdependencies.
- Reframe risk appetite statements to include strategic optionality and adaptive capacity.

Tools: The ROPI Canvas

Use this canvas to map platform investments:

Table 10-4 ROPI Canvas

Element	Key Questions
Stakeholders	Who benefits? Who contributes?
Value Interactions	What flows through the platform?
Strategic Outcomes	What change is enabled?
Infrastructure Linkage	What shared tools or data are activated?
Trust and Legitimacy	How is our reputation and value reinforced?
Sustainability Horizon	What will this unlock in 6, 12, 24 months?

This canvas can support boardroom discussion, grant reporting, and internal planning.

Table 10-5 ROPI Canvas: Member-Led CPD and Mentoring Platform

Element	Key Questions	Example (APHEN Initiative)
Stakeholders	Who benefits? Who contributes?	Benefits: Early-career professionals, experienced mentors, employers
Contributors: Members (content), staff (moderation), partners (framework input)		
Value Interactions	What flows through the platform?	Peer mentoring sessions, CPD webinars, shared case studies, feedback loops
Strategic Outcomes	What change is enabled?	Increased member engagement, career advancement pathways, skills visibility, sector cohesion
Infrastructure Linkage	What shared tools or data are activated?	CRM integration, CPD tracker, digital badges, shared analytics across learning and careers data
Trust and Legitimacy	How is our reputation and value reinforced?	Member-led design process, transparent peer review of CPD content, privacy controls for profiles
Sustainability Horizon	What will this unlock in 6, 12, 24 months?	6 months: Member retention boost
12 months: Employer recognition of mentoring credentials		
24 months: Potential for national credentialing partnership with university or government agency		

How to Use This in Practice

- Boardroom Use: Add this as a standing item in strategic investment discussions to move beyond budget metrics and frame decisions in terms of platform value and alignment.
- Grant Reporting: Use the "Strategic Outcomes" and "Sustainability Horizon" columns to demonstrate systemic impact to funders or partners.
- Internal Planning: Map multiple initiatives side by side using this canvas to prioritise resourcing and track overlapping infrastructure needs.

Case Insight: Credentialing as Platform Asset

Scenario

A mid-sized association invests in a digital micro-credentialing system to recognise emerging skills in a fast-evolving field. The initial goal is to support members' career mobility and signal value to employers.

Platform Investment Timeline:

Year 1: High upfront cost, limited uptake. Most members are unfamiliar with digital credentials. Initial ROI appears negative.

Year 2: External education partners begin embedding credentials in their pathways. Member interest rises. Engagement increases across mentoring and CPD forums.

Year 3: A state government agency adopts the credential as part of a recognised workforce framework. Stakeholder trust and brand value grow substantially.

Year 4: Licensing opportunities emerge with employers and international bodies. The credential becomes a shared infrastructure asset.

Why Traditional ROI Fails

From a conventional ROI perspective, the initiative would appear to underperform in Year 1 and 2. There's no immediate revenue, no offset against cost, and minimal direct user conversion.

How ROPI Reframes the Investment

Table 10-6 How ROPI Reframes the Investment

ROPI Dimension	Observed Value
Reach	Participation expanded from members to partners, employers, and a government body.
Engagement	Credentialing stimulated new CPD pathways, peer mentoring, and employer collaboration.
Value Exchange	Members contributed experience-based learning; employers offered recognition.
Platform Leverage	The credentialing system was reused for spin-out programs and embedded in partner CPD.
Strategic Alignment	Reinforced the association's mission to professionalise the sector and build public trust.

Insight: Traditional ROI would have written off this investment prematurely. A ROPI lens recognises its full lifecycle impact, as an enabler of trust, participation, cross-sector collaboration, and future-ready revenue.

Measuring What Matters Most

Return on Platform Investment (ROPI) is not a replacement for financial scrutiny, it is a strategic enhancement. In platform-based associations, where value is often co-created, cumulative, and distributed across stakeholders, traditional ROI models fall short. They miss the delayed returns of engagement, the infrastructure leverage of shared systems, and the trust dividends earned through alignment with purpose.

ROPI fills that gap. It provides a structured, forward-looking way to evaluate whether platform investments are truly advancing mission, enabling participation, and building adaptive capacity.

By measuring what matters, even when it is indirect, delayed, or intangible, associations can avoid the short-termism that erodes trust and underinvests in infrastructure. They gain a more complete picture of how their platforms create public value, empower members, and position the organisation for future opportunity.

As associations shift from delivering programs to orchestrating ecosystems, ROPI becomes more than a reporting tool, it becomes a strategic compass.

The next part of the book turns to governance, examining how governance systems can either unlock or constrain platform performance, and how agile, risk-aligned oversight can help associations realise the full value of their evolving economic models.

See Chapter 21 for in-depth modelling approaches.

PART III Governance as Economic Infrastructure

This section brings together the economic logic, financial modelling tools, governance diagnostics, and analytical methods that underpin platform success in the association sector. While earlier chapters explored strategy, governance, and capability-building, this part equips association leaders with the economic and structural frameworks needed to make confident, data-driven decisions.

As associations evolve from service providers to platform orchestrators, the economics of scale, value creation, and revenue design also change. These annexures offer board-ready guidance and theoretical rigour to help decision-makers manage that shift.

Chapter 11. Governing for Performance: Economics of Oversight

Governance is More Than Oversight

Governance in most associations is still conceptualised as a compliance function, a system of rules, roles, and rituals designed to prevent failure. But for platform-based associations, that narrow view is insufficient. Governance is not just about risk management, it is about *value enablement*.

This chapter reframes governance as a core economic function: one that reduces coordination costs, manages externalities, allocates decision rights, and sustains trust in multi-actor environments. We position governance not as a constraint on strategy, but as the infrastructure that makes platform strategy possible.

Nobel Prize winner, Ronald Coase's foundational insight, that firms exist to reduce the transaction costs of market exchange, provides a powerful lens through which to understand governance. In the context of associations, governance is not merely a matter of compliance or oversight. It is an economic function: the means by which organisations minimise the cost of coordinating action, managing uncertainty, and sustaining cooperation across diverse actors. This is especially vital in multi-sided association platforms, where value is co-created, not centrally delivered.

Following Oliver Williamson's extension of Coasean logic (Williamson also won the Nobel Prize), governance structures serve to mitigate three key forms of transaction cost: *search and information costs* (who does what?), *bargaining and decision costs* (how do we decide?), and *monitoring and enforcement costs* (how do we know it happened, and what if it doesn't?).

In associations, these costs manifest not only between the organisation and its external stakeholders, but also internally, across the board–executive interface, between departments, and within multi-stakeholder projects.

Governance, then, plays a vital economic role in reducing friction across these domains. Effective governance reduces the cost of collective action by:

- Clarifying roles and expectations between board, staff, members, and external partners.
- Establishing shared decision rules to avoid ambiguity in complex or multi-stakeholder initiatives.
- Preventing duplication, delay, and paralysis by creating efficient mechanisms for delegation and dispute resolution.
- Providing credible commitments through transparent processes and policy coherence that reduce the need for costly renegotiation.

These governance functions substitute for the high costs of repeated negotiation, miscommunication, and conflict resolution. Without them, association operations are burdened by what Williamson called *maladaptation costs,* the cumulative drag of incoherence, uncertainty, or opportunism.

Example: Governance Drag vs Governance Lift

When the *Digital Health Alliance* launched a multi-stakeholder innovation platform, early engagement was strong, but monetisation stalled. Despite demand for premium tools and data products, uptake lagged. A deeper review revealed the issue wasn't financial, it was *governance.*

Decision bottlenecks, unclear data rights, and limited member voice in strategy were slowing down value creation. By redesigning their governance model, introducing a data oversight committee, delegating platform approvals, and embedding participation pathways, they anticipated immediate results:

- An increase in premium service uptake
- Faster approval of innovation pilots
- Stronger member and sponsor trust

Lesson: In platform associations, governance is not a cost, it's the architecture that enables scale, participation, and return on investment.

Governance in Platform Contexts

In platform-based associations, the need for transaction cost management becomes even more pronounced. Value is not delivered top-down, but emerges from the interaction of many actors: members, learners, educators, partners, and even regulators. This creates new kinds of coordination problems: Who has access? Who decides? What happens when roles or interests conflict?

In this context, governance becomes the *invisible architecture* that holds complexity in alignment. It serves as the operating system of the platform, mediating trust, enabling interoperability, and reducing the need for bespoke agreements at every node.

For example:

- In a peer-to-peer mentoring initiative, governance sets the match criteria, feedback channels, and dispute pathways, replacing the need for individual negotiation.
- In a shared credentialing system, governance ensures common standards, auditability, and mutual recognition, lowering the search and credibility costs for users and employers.
- In partner networks, governance formalises participation tiers, decision rights, and value-sharing mechanisms, minimising the ambiguity that would otherwise require constant renegotiation.

Without such governance scaffolding, platform ecosystems either collapse under the weight of coordination failure or devolve into opportunistic behaviour that erodes trust and value.

Governance, properly understood, is not a cost centre, it is a cost *saver*. It reduces friction, lowers the economic barriers to participation, and enables strategic clarity across complex systems of interaction. In platform associations, this role is not peripheral, it is central. Governance becomes the infrastructure that supports exchange, maintains coherence, and makes sustained collaboration economically viable.

The Strategic Functions of Governance in Platform Associations

In traditional associations, governance has often been treated as a compliance function, primarily focused on oversight, accountability, and the minimisation of legal or reputational risk. But in the platform association model, this understanding is incomplete. Governance is not just about control, it is about coordination, coherence, and value enablement. It is the mechanism by which associations steward complex ecosystems, align incentives, manage distributed authority, and protect their legitimacy in dynamic environments.

When reconceptualised through an economic lens, governance performs five interlinked strategic functions that are essential to platform success:

Table 11-1 Strategic Functions of Governance

Function	Description
Coordination	Reduces friction in multi-actor decisions and program delivery
Delegation	Allocates decision rights across executive, platform, and stakeholder layers
Legitimacy Stewardship	Sustains member trust and public confidence in a participatory ecosystem
Risk Differentiation	Distinguishes innovation risk from compliance or reputational risk
Platform Coherence	Ensures that the association's tech, data, and engagement align strategically

Let us examine each function more closely:

1. Coordination

Platform associations operate as multi-sided systems in which value is generated not just by internal teams but through the interaction of members, learners, partners, and data flows. Without clear governance, coordination costs spiral. Delays emerge, duplication proliferates, and decision-making becomes paralysed. Governance, in this sense, is the infrastructure of alignment, providing protocols, participation rules, and collaborative scaffolding that reduce transaction costs and enable distributed action.

2. Delegation

In adaptive platforms, not every decision can or should be escalated to the board. Strategic governance requires clarity about where authority sits, not just between board and executive, but across platform functions such as credentialing, partnerships, or data systems, and within member-led initiatives. Delegated authority frameworks ensure that decisions are made at the appropriate level by those with the right visibility and mandate, while preserving oversight and alignment with broader strategic goals.

3. Legitimacy Stewardship

Associations trade in trust. Unlike commercial platforms, they often carry a normative mandate to represent, serve, or advocate for a professional or public interest. As such, their legitimacy must be continually earned through transparent governance, equitable participation, and integrity of decision-making. In a platform context, where members can see, challenge, and contribute to outcomes, governance becomes a strategic instrument for reinforcing trust, accountability, and legitimacy at scale.

4. Risk Differentiation

A key governance challenge in modern associations is distinguishing between productive uncertainty, such as innovation and experimentation, and exposure risk, such as regulatory breach or reputational harm. Governance must enable exploration and innovation while protecting the organisation's credibility. This requires differentiated oversight mechanisms including risk matrices, innovation sandboxes, and ethical review processes that match the nature and intensity of specific risk domains.

5. Platform Coherence

In a platform-based model, strategy is not executed through linear plans. It emerges through dynamic interactions across technology, data, services, and member engagement. Governance must therefore act as the strategic integrator, ensuring that product development, data use, service design, and monetisation approaches are coherent, aligned, and purpose-driven. Without this coherence function, platform associations risk fragmentation, redundancy, or erosion of trust.

From Control to Value Management

Together, these five functions reposition governance as more than oversight. In platform associations, governance operates as a value management system, supporting alignment, enabling trust, and managing complexity in distributed systems.

Boards must move beyond viewing governance as a constraint. Instead, they should see it as a source of strategic advantage. This shift requires new capabilities including systems thinking, insight into digital risk and trust, and a clear understanding of how governance architecture can shape outcomes.

Governance is no longer a rear-view function. It is a forward-facing design tool that enables the association to manage value, complexity, and legitimacy in a changing environment.

Governance is not just about control, it is about coordination, coherence, and value enablement.

Platform-in-Practice Box: Adaptive Governance in Action

The Australian Learning Exchange (ALE) uses real-time engagement dashboards to inform its board's strategy sessions. By linking participation data with governance indicators, ALE has shifted its meetings from passive reporting to active foresight, aligning board agendas with emerging signals and reducing lag in strategic decisions.

Common Governance Frictions and Economic Impacts

Without adaptive governance structures, platform associations often experience forms of structural drag that reduce their ability to act with speed, alignment, or strategic clarity. These frictions are not just procedural issues. They impose real economic costs, in the form of delayed initiatives, duplicated effort, missed opportunities, and diminished member trust.

Some of the most common governance frictions in platform associations include:

- **Duplication of authority:** When two teams, committees, or working groups claim overlapping responsibility for a decision, uncertainty increases and progress slows. This leads to redundant effort, stakeholder confusion, and inconsistent execution.
- **Over-centralisation:** Boards that retain control over tactical or operational decisions often become bottlenecks. This results in delayed responses, missed timing windows, and disempowerment of executive teams, all of which increase coordination costs.
- **Under-delegation:** When staff are unclear about their authority or are working under outdated delegation frameworks, innovation slows and execution risk increases. Teams wait for sign-off on matters that should be resolved at lower levels of decision-making
- **No Staff:** When there are insufficient appropriately capable staff.
- **Token stakeholder input:** Seeking feedback without a clear pathway for influence erodes trust. When members or partners perceive consultation as

symbolic rather than substantive, engagement declines, and reputational risk grows.[7]

- **Misalignment between technology and governance:** Platform tools, data systems, or AI-powered features often evolve faster than the policies and governance mechanisms that oversee them. This creates ethical and operational risk, especially where automation affects member experience or decision transparency.

Each of these frictions contributes to inefficiency and erodes the overall platform experience. They increase internal coordination costs and reduce the association's ability to generate value through its ecosystem.

In economic terms, governance becomes a liability when it fails to manage transaction costs effectively. Instead of supporting strategic flow, poor governance architecture introduces friction, delay, and incoherence, turning what should be an enabler into a hidden cost centre.

The challenge for boards and executives is to identify and resolve these frictions before they escalate into conflict or institutional drift. Governance must be continuously reviewed and designed to support the association's evolving strategy, stakeholder expectations, and technology environment.

Economic Governance Officer

As associations move from traditional hierarchies to platform ecosystems, the Company Secretary plays a central role in enabling coordination, clarifying authority, and supporting strategic coherence. This role is increasingly vital in environments where governance decisions must balance speed, legitimacy, and complexity.

In the platform association model, the role of the Company Secretary must evolve from procedural compliance or statutory obligations to a governance economist, a strategic actor who ensures that governance structures are efficient, adaptive, and aligned with the organisation's value logic.

The Company Secretary contributes to economic performance by:

- **Mapping and aligning decision rights:** The Secretary ensures that decision-making authority is clearly defined, consistent with legal obligations, and cost-aligned. This includes clarifying what decisions belong at board level, what is appropriately delegated to executives, and what may be shared with platform participants or partners.
- **Maintaining responsive delegation frameworks:** Delegation should reflect strategic priorities and operational needs. The Secretary ensures that delegation instruments are current and scalable, so that authority can flow to the right level without unnecessary escalation or bottlenecks.

---

[7] See: Arnstein, S. R. (1969). A Ladder of Citizen Participation. *Journal of the American Planning Association*, 35(4), 216 - 224. http://www.informaworld.com/10.1080/01944366908977225

- **Designing insight-focused reporting:** Traditional reporting often emphasises compliance and past performance. The Company Secretary can support more strategic governance by embedding forward-looking indicators, risk intelligence, and value-related metrics into board and committee reporting processes.
- **Aligning governance rituals with strategy:** Agendas, meeting cycles, committee structures, and review mechanisms should reinforce strategic clarity, not preserve inertia. The Secretary acts as a design steward, ensuring these governance practices remain focused on decision quality, stakeholder alignment, and directional learning.

This reframing positions the Company Secretary as a key custodian of institutional coherence. They help reduce governance friction, support legitimacy, and ensure that governance enables rather than impedes organisational performance. In platform associations, this role is not just administrative. It is foundational to the association's ability to govern complexity, create value, and sustain member trust.

Why Dual-Hatting the Company Secretary Role Undermines Good Governance

In many associations, the Company Secretary role is informally combined with another executive position, such as the CEO, CFO, or Chief Operating Officer. While this practice may appear efficient or pragmatic, it introduces serious governance risks. This is often referred to as "dual-hatting".

Dual-hatting undermines the independence and objectivity required of the Company Secretary. This role is responsible for advising the board on governance matters, maintaining procedural integrity, and ensuring that board decisions are informed, lawful, and accountable. When the same individual is also responsible for operational execution, performance reporting, or strategic delivery, this creates an inherent conflict of interest.

Key risks of dual-hatting include:

- **Loss of governance independence:** The Company Secretary must be able to raise concerns, identify gaps in reporting, and ensure that board processes are followed without fear of undermining their own executive performance.
- **Dilution of the governance function:** When combined with operational responsibilities, the governance role is often deprioritised or treated as an administrative afterthought. This weakens the organisation's ability to maintain governance quality during periods of growth, risk, or complexity.
- **Reduced trust and clarity for directors:** Directors rely on the Company Secretary as a neutral advisor. If that person is also part of the executive leadership team being held to account, it can compromise confidence in the governance process and blur the lines of accountability.

Good governance requires clear role separation and institutional checks that ensure advice to the board is independent of management interest. The Company Secretary must have sufficient standing, access, and independence to perform this role effectively. Boards should actively avoid dual-hatting arrangements and instead recognise the Secretary as a distinct and strategic position within the governance system.

Governance Alignment and the APSF

Governance is one of the three foundational design pillars in the *Association Platform Success Framework* (APSF), alongside strategy and technology. In a platform-based association, governance is not just about oversight. It is the mechanism by which participation, data, innovation, and interoperability are managed with legitimacy and strategic coherence.

Figure 11.1 *Association Platform Success Framework*

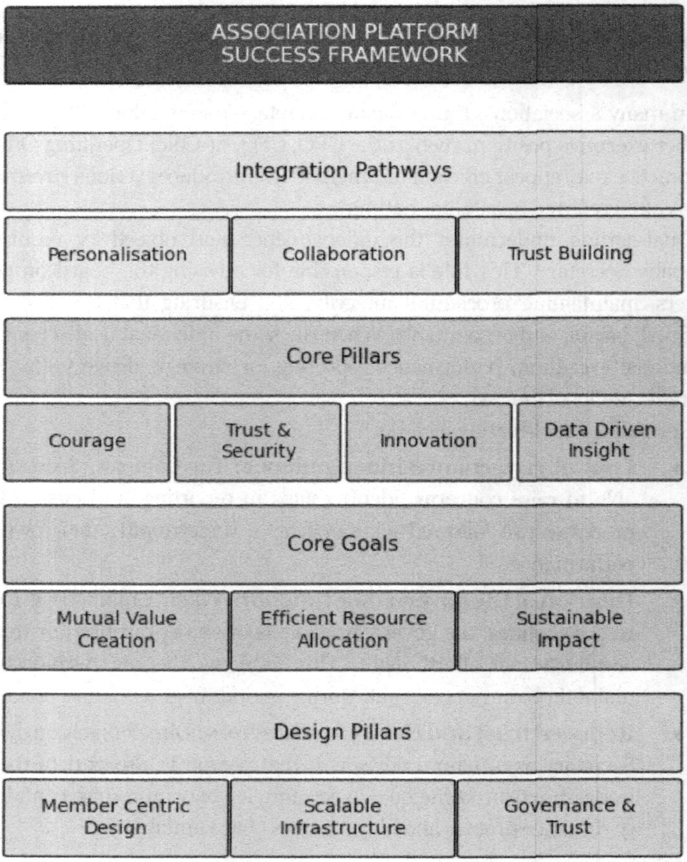

When governance is well-designed and aligned with the APSF, it enables four critical domains of institutional performance:

- **Participation governance:** Members need clarity about how their voice influences decisions, contributes to outcomes, and shapes the direction of the association. This requires transparent processes, clear pathways for engagement, and feedback loops that demonstrate impact.
- **Data governance:** Boards must ensure that data collected through the platform is used ethically, securely, and in alignment with strategic goals. This includes clarity on consent, value exchange, and data-driven decision-making that respects member trust.
- **Innovation governance:** Experimentation must be supported, but not unmanaged. Good governance helps distinguish between acceptable uncertainty and unacceptable risk. This allows the association to test new ideas, partnerships, or technologies without exposing the organisation to reputational or compliance failures.
- **Interoperability governance:** The association's technology stack must support integration with partners, platforms, and third-party tools. Governance ensures these decisions are not driven solely by short-term operational needs but are aligned with broader ecosystem goals and standards.

When these governance domains are integrated into the APSF, the association is better positioned to lead, adapt, and scale. However, when they are disconnected or underdeveloped, the board may become a source of drag rather than a steward of strategic transformation.

Alignment across these domains requires deliberate design. Boards must treat governance not as a legacy structure to be maintained, but as a living system to be architected, evaluated, and continuously improved.

Governance Maturity as Economic Capacity

In platform-based associations governance is not merely a matter of oversight. It is an economic function. The way an association allocates decision rights, manages risk, structures trust, and governs participation directly shapes its capacity to generate, retain, and distribute value. Governance maturity, in this context, is not just a compliance indicator. It serves as a proxy for the organisation's economic capability because it reflects how well the association can coordinate complexity, adapt to change, and steward value across its ecosystem.

From Compliance to Coherence: A Maturity Lens

As outlined in *The Modern Association Playbook* governance maturity can be understood as a developmental spectrum. This spectrum reflects how well an association's governance system is aligned with its strategic complexity, stakeholder expectations, and value model.

Governance maturity progresses through three stages:

- **Foundational:** Governance is focused on basic compliance, procedural rigour, and clear separation of roles. Risk is managed through formal structures and reporting, with limited agility or foresight.
- **Strategic:** Governance integrates performance oversight with purpose, values, and adaptive decision-making. The board begins to function as a strategic asset, engaging with complexity rather than avoiding it.
- **Platform-Enabled:** Governance is embedded within digital infrastructure, stakeholder ecosystems, and distributed intelligence. It supports dynamic coordination, data-informed insight, and value orchestration across networks.

This progression is not cosmetic. It directly determines the association's ability to:

- Monetise participation without undermining trust
- Embed ethical AI and data governance in operational and product design
- Navigate multi-stakeholder environments with legitimacy, responsiveness, and clarity
- Maintain strategic alignment as speed, complexity, and information asymmetry increase

Each level of maturity expands the association's strategic capacity and economic bandwidth. A more mature governance system is not just more accountable. It is more capable of coordinating across systems, responding to feedback, and sustaining value in complex and dynamic environments.

Aligning with ISO 37000, 37004, and 37005

The ISO governance standards provide a powerful scaffolding to frame governance as an enabler of long-term value, economic, social, and institutional.

ISO 37000 – Governance of Organisations

This standard defines governance as the system by which an organisation makes and implements decisions in pursuit of its objectives. It outlines 11 key principles, including:

- **Purpose** (ensuring clarity of public value),
- **Strategy and Oversight** (integrating planning with accountability),
- **Stakeholder Engagement** (aligning governance with legitimacy and trust),
- **Responsiveness and Accountability** (adapting to change without losing coherence).

These principles map directly onto platform logic. In a multi-sided association ecosystem, governance must support *dynamic value coordination*, not just static oversight.

ISO 37004 – Governance Maturity Model

ISO 37004 introduces a staged approach to evaluating and enhancing governance practices. It enables associations to self-assess or audit their:

- **Leadership clarity** (Is governance actively shaping direction?),
- **Transparency and learning cycles** (Is insight being acted upon?),
- **Stakeholder inclusion and ethics** (Are trade-offs visible and shared?),
- **System feedback mechanisms** (Can we detect friction before it becomes conflict?).

This model can be adapted as an **economic maturity scale** for associations, where higher levels of governance maturity directly correlate with:

- Increased member participation and co-creation,
- Ethical monetisation and data governance,
- Effective risk absorption and scenario planning,
- Greater ROI from strategic initiatives.

ISO 37005 – Whistleblowing Management Systems

While seemingly peripheral, ISO 37005 becomes central in the platform context. As associations facilitate more peer-to-peer interaction, the risk of harm, misuse, or exclusion rises. Governance maturity includes the infrastructure to:

- Detect ethical breaches across digital ecosystems,
- Manage voice, grievance, and correction,
- Reinforce psychological safety and institutional integrity, essential ingredients for participation economies.

Governance as a Platform Enabler

In modern associations, economic performance is increasingly dependent on the quality and adaptability of governance. Governance is no longer just a safeguard against failure. It is a platform enabler, a key driver of coordination, legitimacy, and value realisation across ecosystems.

To fulfil this role, governance must be:

- **Adaptive:** Capable of responding to emergent member needs, environmental changes, and systemic disruptions with agility and clarity.
- **Ethical:** Structured to govern data, AI, and monetisation decisions through fair, transparent, and values-aligned processes.
- **Participatory:** Designed to distribute agency across networks, members, and partners, while still maintaining clear lines of accountability.
- **Measurable:** Assessed through meaningful indicators such as trust levels, engagement depth, co-created value, and ecosystem coherence.

Meeting these demands requires a new model of governance maturity. This model must go beyond procedural compliance and integrate international standards, such as ISO 37000, alongside sector-specific diagnostic tools, including the Governance Strain Index and Friction Index. It also requires a cultural shift at board level, from governing solely for risk mitigation to governing for value creation, alignment, and long-term performance.

Platform-enabling governance is not an abstract ideal. It is a practical necessity for associations that aim to lead in dynamic, networked environments.

Diagnosing Governance as Economic Infrastructure

If associations are to thrive as platforms, their governance systems must evolve beyond compliance and oversight. Governance becomes not just an enabler of legitimacy, but a form of infrastructure, one that carries economic value, distributes capability, and shapes institutional resilience. This section introduces a practical framework for diagnosing that infrastructure, linking governance maturity directly to economic performance.

Governance as an Economic Driver

In platform-based associations, every strategic choice, from monetisation to data ethics to partnership models, is governed. The maturity of those governance systems determines not just how decisions are made, but how value is created, sustained, and shared. To operationalise this insight, we propose a diagnostic tool: the *Governance–Economics Maturity Matrix.*

This matrix aligns five critical capabilities with corresponding governance indicators and the economic outcomes they influence. It allows boards and executives to assess whether their current governance arrangements are fit for a platform environment.

Table 11-2 Governance–Economics Maturity Matrix

Capability	Governance Indicator	Economic Implication
Adaptive Decision-Making	Scenario readiness, use of ISO 37004 maturity tools	Increased agility, opportunity capture
Ethical Data Use	Data charter, AI ethics board (ISO 42001 alignment)	Reduced risk of backlash, increased trust
Participation Infrastructure	Stakeholder mapping, inclusive design processes	Higher engagement, more diverse value creation
Insight and Learning Culture	Governance dashboards, sensemaking loops	Better resource allocation, faster pivots
Risk Distribution Capacity	Delegations, ecosystem contracts, whistleblowing systems	Resilience to platform volatility and failure

Reading the Matrix

Each row in the matrix represents a systemic capability required for economic performance in modern associations. The associated governance indicators signal whether that capability is embedded, emerging, or absent.

- **If adaptive decision-making is underdeveloped**, the association may struggle to pivot when market signals or member preferences change.
- **If ethical data use is not actively governed**, trust, the currency of platform models, may erode rapidly in response to privacy breaches or opaque algorithms.
- **If participation infrastructure is limited**, members may revert to passive engagement, reducing co-created value and diminishing return on platform investment (ROPI).
- **If learning cultures are not reflected in governance dashboards**, strategic drift can occur, insights remain unacted on, and misalignment compounds.
- **If risk is overly centralised**, the association may become fragile, overly cautious, or slow to respond to emerging threats.

This diagnostic tool helps association leaders see governance as an economic system, with interdependencies, feedback loops, and leverage points. It also enables targeted interventions, allowing boards to strengthen weak links before they constrain strategic potential.

From Diagnosis to Design

The governance maturity matrix is more than a reflection tool. It serves as a prompt for deliberate and strategic design.

- **In governance reviews**, it can be used to track how current board practices support or inhibit economic performance.
- **In board development agendas**, it links governance capability-building with measurable outcomes such as trust, alignment, and adaptive decision-making.
- **In transformation planning**, it ensures that governance evolves in parallel with changes to the business model, technology stack, and stakeholder expectations.

Crucially, the matrix can be paired with ISO 37004's structured maturity evaluation approach. This allows associations to move beyond anecdotal assessments and towards evidence-based governance design.

By aligning internal governance capability with external complexity, associations can transition from reactive management to proactive orchestration. This is not simply about keeping pace with change, it is about shaping it with intention, legitimacy, and strategic clarity.

From Capability to Coordination: Governance as a System-Level Asset

As platform-based associations grow in complexity, governance cannot remain static. It must evolve into a system-level function, one that coordinates not just internal controls, but external accountability, stakeholder legitimacy, and adaptive alignment across an ecosystem.

Governance as Coordination Infrastructure

In platform environments, the economic value of an association increasingly depends on its ability to manage:

- Competing stakeholder interests,
- Multi-directional value flows,
- Decentralised participation models, and
- Continuous adaptation in the face of technological and societal change.

Governance maturity, therefore, becomes a form of *coordination infrastructure*, enabling the institution to act coherently despite structural complexity. This is where ISO 37000's emphasis on purpose, stakeholder inclusion, and responsiveness becomes essential. These are not aspirational ideals; they are performance requirements.
When applied strategically, mature governance systems:

- Accelerate implementation by reducing friction and ambiguity,
- Increase trust and participation by signalling fairness and clarity,
- Enable scale by delegating authority and embedding feedback mechanisms.

This is the logic behind the inclusion of governance as a driver, not just an enabler, in platform strategy.

Governance Maturity and Return on Platform Investment (ROPI)

The association's ability to generate sustainable economic return from platform activity, its *Return on Platform Investment (ROPI)*, is highly sensitive to governance capability.

A high-ROPI association is one that:

- Anticipates risk through distributed sensing,
- Builds trust through transparent decision-making,
- Encourages co-creation through shared agency,
- Maintains coherence even as new actors and functions are added.

Governance immaturity, by contrast, often correlates with:

- Value leakage (e.g. under-monetised participation),
- Strategic drag (e.g. duplication, misalignment),
- Friction escalation (e.g. poor member experience, reputational exposure).

In this light, governance becomes a *rate-limiting factor* for value creation. Where trust, legitimacy, and coordination are weak, economic potential stalls.

Final Reflections: From Governance to Economic Foresight

The closing imperative for this chapter is clear: governance must no longer be viewed as the slow anchor in a fast-moving environment. Instead, it must be reconceived as an anticipatory system, capable of enabling foresight, surfacing weak signals, and sustaining alignment in periods of flux.

To build this capacity, associations should:

1. **Treat governance as an investment,** one that enables scale, resilience, and adaptation.
2. **Integrate governance diagnostics with economic planning**, using tools like the Governance–Economics Maturity Matrix, ISO 37004 maturity models, and the Friction Index.
3. **Embed reflexivity** into governance cycles, through regular board self-evaluation, member engagement reviews, and ethical oversight mechanisms.
4. **Design for participation**, not just compliance. Economic returns increasingly flow from trust-based interaction, not control-based transactions.

As we transition to *Part IV*, we move from governance systems to economic design at the sector and ecosystem level, where associations operate not just as individual organisations, but as public value platforms embedded in broader systems of capability, legitimacy, and coordination.

Case: PNA's Governance Reset as an Economic Strategy

Late in the year, the Professional Network Association (PNA) faced a critical challenge. Its new "Network Futures" platform, designed to enable member-led ecosystems and sector-wide collaboration, had launched with strong uptake, but uneven results. Engagement data showed spikes of activity followed by sudden drop-offs. Sponsorship interest was growing, but governance approvals lagged. And cross-sector project partnerships were stalling in complexity.

The CEO, Claire Evans, initiated a governance maturity review, not as a compliance exercise, but as an economic reset.

What they found:

- Governance was still structured around legacy committee hierarchies, slowing cross-functional coordination.
- The board lacked visibility of where platform risk, particularly data use and co-branding, was being created.
- Members contributing significant value (e.g. open-access resources, peer mentoring) had little voice in strategic decisions.

Working with a governance advisor, PNA applied a Governance–Economics Maturity Matrix across key dimensions. They paired it with ISO 37004-aligned maturity indicators and mapped platform-related risks using a custom friction diagnostic.

Actions taken:

- Created a new Platform Oversight Subcommittee, blending board members with external digital and ethics advisors.
- Introduced governance dashboards to track engagement health, value co-creation hotspots, and early risk signals.
- Shifted delegations of authority to support faster pilot approvals and member-driven project launches.
- Developed a Digital Ethics Charter based on ISO 37000 principles, co-designed with members and sponsors.

Outcomes:

- New monetisation experiments (e.g. a data-driven mentoring match tool) launched faster and with clearer accountability.
- Member satisfaction and trust metrics improved, particularly around decision transparency.
- Board agendas shifted from reporting to scenario-based foresight, using engagement and platform performance data as strategic signals.

By viewing governance as economic infrastructure, PNA moved beyond crisis management to capability building. Their ROPI improved not just through better platform design, but through governance maturity as a strategic asset.

Summary: Economics of Oversight and Alignment

1. Governance Is Economic Infrastructure: Governance is not just compliance, it is the infrastructure that enables coordination, reduces friction, and stewards trust in platform-based associations. It directly influences how value is created, shared, and protected.

2. Governance Reduces Transaction Costs: Clarity of roles, delegated authority, and structured decision pathways reduce duplication, delay, and ambiguity, all of which are hidden costs in multi-actor ecosystems.

3. Five Strategic Functions Define Platform Governance: Effective governance in platform associations must manage:

- Coordination
- Delegation
- Legitimacy stewardship
- Risk differentiation

- Platform coherence

These functions enable the platform to scale while staying aligned with purpose and trust

4. Governance Maturity = Economic Capability: Mature governance systems can absorb risk, enable participation, and support innovation. Weak systems become bottlenecks. The Governance–Economics Maturity Matrix links governance capability directly to economic outcomes like agility, trust, and return on platform investment (ROPI).

5. The Company Secretary as Governance Economist: The modern Company Secretary is not just a compliance monitor, but a strategist, ensuring decision rights, data ethics, and risk frameworks align with organisational value flows.

6. Aligning with ISO 37000, 37004, 37005: ISO standards provide a globally recognised governance framework that supports strategic coherence, performance monitoring, ethical oversight, and stakeholder legitimacy, essential for digital and ecosystem-aligned associations.

7. Governance Enables ROPI: Return on Platform Investment is tied to how well governance systems anticipate risk, maintain coherence, and enable value co-creation. Governance must be designed for foresight, not just control.

Tool: Governance Maturity Self-Assessment Tool

Aligning Governance Capabilities with Economic Performance

Instructions:

Rate your association on each of the five governance capabilities below using the following scale:

- ☐ **Emerging** – Largely ad hoc, unclear, or underdeveloped
- ☐ **Developing** – Some structure in place but inconsistent or siloed
- ☐ **Embedded** – Integrated into decision-making and strategy

For each capability, use the prompts to guide discussion. Identify priority areas for improvement.

Table 11-3 Governance Maturity Self-Assessment Tool

Capability	Assessment Prompts	Rating	Notes / Actions
1. Adaptive Decision-Making	- Do we use scenario planning or foresight tools at board level? - Are governance settings regularly reviewed for responsiveness? - Is ISO 37004 or similar used for maturity mapping?	☐/☐/☐	
2. Ethical Data Use	- Do we have a data ethics charter or AI use policy? - Are decisions about data governance reviewed independently? - Are we aligned with ISO 42001 principles?	☐/☐/☐	
3. Participation Infrastructure	- Do stakeholders have clear channels for input and co-decision-making? - Are our rules inclusive by design? - Do we actively govern engagement equity?	☐/☐/☐	
4. Insight and Learning Culture	- Are we using engagement and platform performance dashboards? - Do we act on feedback loops? - Are governance decisions data-informed?	☐/☐/☐	
5. Risk Distribution Capacity	- Do we have delegations that empower local/pilot innovation? - Do we use contracts or charters to share risk in partnerships? - Do we have accessible grievance mechanisms (ISO 37005)?	☐/☐/☐	

Summary Reflection:

- Which two areas are your strongest?
- Which one represents the biggest risk or drag on platform performance?

Chapter 12. Strategic Metrics for Platform Maturity

What Gets Measured Still Gets Misunderstood

Associations have never lacked for metrics. Attendance rates, CPD hours, membership churn, satisfaction surveys are staples of board reporting. But in a platform context, many of these metrics are either lagging indicators or blind spots.

Measuring platform maturity requires more than counting outputs. It means tracking contribution, interaction, flow, trust, and system readiness. This chapter introduces a multidimensional metrics framework that helps association leaders assess transformation progress, align strategy with platform logic, and evaluate performance beyond legacy indicators.

The Problem with Legacy Metrics

Legacy metrics focus on internal delivery:

Table 12-1 Legacy Metrics

Legacy Metric	Limitation in Platform Context
Event Attendance	Doesn't track long-term engagement or peer learning impact
Member Retention	Misses network value created by non-members or transient users
Revenue per Member	Obscures cross-subsidy and indirect monetisation dynamics
Survey Satisfaction	Often lagging, hard to correlate with system performance

These metrics treat members as consumers, not contributors or co-creators.

From Activity to Maturity: Rethinking What Matters

Platform maturity is measured not by size, but by adaptive capacity, systemic value, and participatory flow. The key shift is from tracking activity to measuring enablement. There are four core metric categories:

Table 12-2 Four Core Measures

Metric Category	Focus	Why It Matters
Reach & Engagement	Network density, contribution rates	Indicates platform relevance and energy

Metric Category	Focus	Why It Matters
Value Creation	Exchange volume, peer interaction	Tracks co-production, not just consumption
Infrastructure Maturity	Interoperability, data reuse	Shows efficiency and ability to scale
Trust & Legitimacy	Perceived fairness, ethics, inclusion	Core to sustainable engagement and ecosystem growth

The Platform Performance Scorecard (PPS)

This tool provides a structured way to track metrics across platform maturity dimensions.

Table 12-3 Platform Performance Scorecard (Illustrative)

Domain	Key Metric	Current Value	Target	Trend
Participation Depth	% of members contributing content	34%	50%	↑
Interaction Frequency	Avg. monthly peer interactions per user	2.1	4.0	→
Cross-Sector Linkage	# of partner orgs sharing platform data	5	12	↑
Content Reuse Rate	% of resources accessed >3 times	47%	60%	→
Governance Trust Index	Stakeholder trust score (survey)	68%	80%	↓
Time to Decision	Avg. time from initiative proposal to approval	45 days	20 days	↑

Boards should use this scorecard to anchor discussion, align decision-making, and diagnose maturity gaps.

Leading vs Lagging Metrics

Table 12-4 Metrics by type

Metric Type	Characteristics	Example
Lagging	Historical, output-focused	Retention, past revenue
Leading	Predictive, activity-focused	Contribution rate, early drop-off
Diagnostic	Pattern-focused, identifies frictions	Time to decision, escalation rate
Relational	Captures trust, inclusion, or perception	NPS, qualitative insight

Associations should balance all four types, especially to track transformation progress over time.

Embedding Metrics in Board Governance

Strategic metrics should not live only in operations and must shape board conversations. This means:

- Including platform metrics in CEO reports and strategy reviews
- Using dashboards aligned to strategic priorities (e.g. APSF, ROPI, monetisation maturity)
- Embedding metric review in risk appetite statements and adaptive governance protocols
- Ensuring that performance dashboards show flow, not just static results

Boards should also ask: *What are we not seeing?* Silence in a key metric area (e.g. member-led innovation) may signal design failure.

Case Application: Metrics for CPD Redesign

An association shifting from in-person CPD events to a platform-based microlearning system might track:

Table 12-5 Metrics example

New Metric	Why It Matters
% of CPD completed on mobile	Accessibility and modality relevance
Repeat learner rate	Signals value of content and platform experience
Peer-to-peer recommendation	Captures advocacy and trust
CPD credit velocity	Measures flow rather than volume
User satisfaction with design	Feedback on interface, agency, and flow

Legacy metrics (e.g. number of webinars) miss all of this.

Using Metrics to Drive Cultural Change

Well-designed metrics are signals of what matters. Associations that measure contribution, alignment, or ethical design send a message that:

- Value is co-created
- Strategy is adaptive
- Engagement is participatory
- Governance is accountable

Metrics can legitimise transformation, or undermine it if poorly chosen.

Metrics That Move the Mission

For platform-based associations, the challenge is no longer just to measure more. It is to measure *differently*. Strategic metrics must reflect the underlying logic of interaction, enablement, and ecosystem stewardship.

The next chapter will build on this by exploring how associations can apply *portfolio thinking* and innovation risk models to their investment strategy, treating programs not as stand-alone activities, but as elements in a dynamic, strategic system.

Chapter 13. Portfolio Thinking and the Economics of Innovation Risk

From Projects to Portfolios

Most associations still manage programs as isolated initiatives with their own budget, team, and risk profile. But in a platform context, this model breaks down. Projects interact, compete for resources, overlap in purpose, and often succeed or fail based on *systemic interdependencies.*

To navigate this complexity, associations must shift from project thinking to *portfolio thinking.* This chapter introduces the logic and tools of innovation portfolio management which is grounded in economics, risk theory, and platform design. It shows how to apply it to transformation initiatives, service redesign, and venture development in modern associations.

Why Portfolio Thinking Matters for Associations

Innovation is no longer a siloed activity. It is the engine of sustainability, legitimacy, and future relevance. But innovation comes with uncertainty, and uncertainty is a governance and investment challenge.

Portfolio thinking helps associations:

- Manage strategic bets and long-cycle returns
- Balance mission delivery with commercial experimentation
- Allocate capital and attention across **risk types**, not just departments
- Avoid **innovation fatigue** by clarifying what's exploratory vs core

Types of Innovation in Platform Associations

Type of Innovation	Example in Associations	Risk Profile
Core Enhancements	New CPD formats, improved CRM features	Low to medium
Adjacent Initiatives	Piloting services for non-member stakeholders	Medium
Transformational Bets	New revenue models, platform spinouts	High

Each type requires different metrics, risk appetite, and governance oversight.

Managing Risk Like an Economist

Innovation is often described in binary terms: success or failure. But economics views innovation more probabilistically. Risk is not just about downside; it's about distribution of outcomes and optionality.

Key ideas for associations:

- **Expected Value**: Even if many pilots fail, a few high-return initiatives may justify total investment.
- **Strategic Optionality**: Some investments create future options, even if initial returns are small.
- **Failure by Design**: Well-scoped pilots that fail quickly and cheaply are a sign of health, not failure.

Portfolio Structure and Composition

A healthy innovation portfolio balances across four key dimensions:

Dimension	Considerations
Time Horizon	Short-term wins vs long-term transformation
Risk Type	Market risk, stakeholder risk, technical risk
Value Type	Economic return, social impact, reputational advantage
Governance Intensity	High-touch board oversight vs sandboxed experimentation

Boards should review portfolio composition annually as part of strategic risk management.

Investment Allocation by Risk Profile

Risk Tier	Governance Response	Funding Principle
Low Risk	Operational management	Baseline budget
Moderate Risk	CEO + Executive Committee oversight	Strategic program envelope
High Risk	Board-level authorisation and milestone gates	Ringfenced capital or venture arm

This framework ensures innovation is safe to try without being unsafe to ignore.

Innovation Accounting: Tracking Portfolio Performance

Beyond financial ROI, associations should track:

- **Time-to-learning**: How quickly are insights generated?
- **Iteration velocity**: How many adaptive cycles per initiative?

- **Portfolio balance**: Ratio of incremental to disruptive experiments
- **Kill rate**: Are underperforming pilots being retired appropriately?

These metrics ensure that innovation is both intentional and adaptive, not opportunistic or reactive.

Real-World Application: PNA Innovation Portfolio

The fictional *Professional Network Association (PNA)* adopted portfolio logic to manage:

- A mobile-first CPD redesign (low risk, adjacent)
- A digital mentoring marketplace (moderate risk, user dependent)
- A spin-out social enterprise providing credentialing tools to small nonprofits (high risk, transformational)

Using a visual dashboard, PNA's board reviewed strategic alignment, risk distribution, and budget balance. Result: more focused investment, clearer kill criteria, and stronger engagement from staff.

Governance Implications and Capability

Boards must evolve their mindset from "approving projects" to curating innovation systems. This means having a portfolio lens in strategic planning sessions:

- Delegating *bounded risk* to executives while owning systemic risk
- Embedding innovation metrics in board reporting
- Treating failure as learning, not liability, when within defined bounds

The Company Secretary and governance team play a key role in translating innovation risk into appropriate oversight structures, ensuring alignment between exploration and accountability.

Curate, Don't Just Approve

Innovation is not a series of isolated ideas; it is a systemic capability. For associations navigating transformation, the goal is not to avoid failure, but to design for risk-managed exploration. This approach is captured in Figure 13.1 which illustrates the Innovation Portfolio Balance Matrix.

Figure 13.1 maps three innovation types, Core Enhancements, Adjacent Initiatives, and Transformational Bets, against risk and time horizon. It offers a visual guide for boards to assess whether their innovation investments are appropriately balanced across short-term certainty and long-term potential.

Portfolio thinking empowers boards and executives to:

- Maintain continuity in today's core delivery
- Support adjacent innovation - that is, invest in opportunities that stretch existing strengths into new but related domains. This may include launching pilot programs, expanding into adjacent member needs, or rethinking

service delivery formats. While less risky than transformational bets, adjacent innovation demands active support and strategic space to test, learn, and adapt.

- Make room for bold, transformational bets that shape the future

Board and Governance Implications

From a governance perspective, adjacent innovation often:

- Requires moderate resourcing and clear decision rights
- Calls for oversight mechanisms that track early signals of relevance or traction
- Involves member or customer input loops to ensure alignment with emerging expectations

As we transition to Chapter 14, we scale this view outward, examining how associations can shift from financial sustainability to systemic contribution and mission-based return on investment (ROI). This includes redefining success in terms of public value and long-term legitimacy.

Figure 13.1 Innovation portfolio

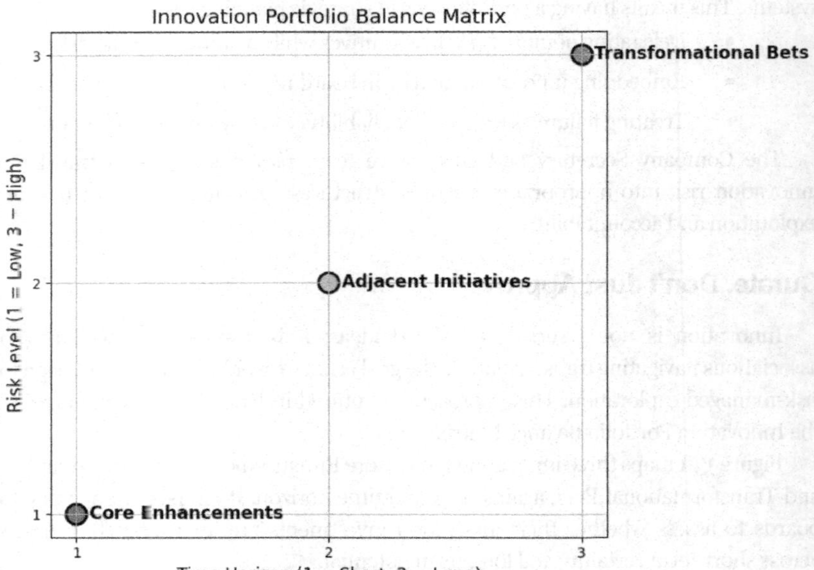

Chapter 14. From Financial Sustainability to Systemic Contribution

Moving the Goalposts

For decades, the strategic benchmark for most associations was financial sustainability. Could they balance the budget? Retain members? Deliver services within their means? These questions are still relevant, but no longer sufficient.

In a platform-enabled world, associations are not just service providers. They are ecosystem orchestrators, data stewards, and public value actors. Their impact reaches far beyond internal operations, and so too must their definition of success.

This chapter introduces a framework for assessing *systemic contribution* across economic, social, and institutional value, created by platform-based associations. It invites boards to move beyond survival thinking and reframe their organisations as public-purpose infrastructures.

From Inputs to Impact: Expanding the Value Frame

Table 14-1 Traditional association value models were inward-facing:

Value Dimension	Traditional View	Expanded View
Financial Health	Budget balance, cash reserves	Long-term reinvestment capacity
Member Engagement	Attendance, dues	Contribution, co-design, knowledge sharing
Advocacy Outcomes	Wins in policy or funding	Enabling systemic reform or institutional trust
Learning Delivery	CPD units offered	Capability uplift across systems and sectors

Systemic contribution asks: *What changes because we exist?* Not just for members, but for society, institutions, and future readiness.

Three Domains of Systemic Contribution

In a platform-enabled world, the true worth of an association cannot be reduced to member benefits or service delivery. Instead, modern associations must be recognised for the systemic value they generate, value that is co-produced, distributed across ecosystems, and catalytic in nature.

This broader conception of contribution can be grouped into three interdependent domains: Economic Value, Social Value, and Institutional Value. Each represents a sphere of impact that extends well beyond traditional return-on-investment (ROI) metrics, and positions associations as essential infrastructure for 21st-century challenges.

Economic Value: Enabling Ecosystems, Capabilities, and Innovation

Ecosystem Enablement

Modern associations are uniquely positioned to act as neutral infrastructure providers within complex ecosystems. By coordinating shared data standards, interoperability frameworks, or procurement baselines, they unlock collective efficiency and reduce fragmentation. This is not about owning platforms, it's about enabling trusted interoperability between industry, education, and policy actors.

Example: A national engineering association standardises digital credentialing formats, enabling members to move seamlessly between projects, employers, and jurisdictions, and facilitating workforce mobility across the sector.

Industry Capability Uplift

Associations can serve as strategic capability-builders through the development of learning pathways, microcredentials, and member-led knowledge systems. These efforts do not just benefit individuals, they lift the baseline of industry readiness and competitiveness.

Example: A creative industries body launches an AI-readiness academy co-designed with tech providers, training members in ethical deployment and interdisciplinary collaboration, directly addressing sector-wide capability gaps.

Innovation Acceleration

By harnessing their community of practitioners, associations can become innovation catalysts, curating problem-solving challenges, innovation grants, or member-contributed policy pilots. Innovation becomes distributed and embedded, not outsourced or centralised.

Example: A rural health association launches an open innovation call for member-led solutions to telehealth access, resulting in a new triage protocol that is adopted nationally.

Social Value: Building Inclusion, Cohesion, and Cultural Legitimacy

Inclusion and Access

Associations can serve as gateways to opportunity for underrepresented or marginalised groups. By designing alternate entry pathways, recognising non-traditional credentials, and rethinking membership models, they extend the benefits of professional and civic participation.

Example: A legal association partners with First Nations educators to co-design a mentorship and pathway program for Indigenous students entering the profession, with the association underwriting course navigation, tutoring, and cultural support.

Community Cohesion

In an era of declining institutional trust and rising polarisation, associations offer a middle space for deliberation, solidarity, and shared norms. Their strength lies in convening diverse views around shared practice, not ideology.

Example: A national social work body creates moderated, peer-led online forums to tackle ethical dilemmas, not as policy directives, but as a living community of values negotiation.

Cultural Legitimacy

Representation matters. Associations that proactively diversify leadership, reflect the lived realities of their field, and elevate new voices do not just look different, they become more credible, responsive, and resilient.

Example: A science association publishes annual board diversity metrics and institutes rotating "emerging leader" observer roles, giving early-career professionals and underrepresented groups visible roles in governance.

Institutional Value: Stewarding Trust, Insight, and Policy Responsiveness

Trust Infrastructure

As member-driven bodies, associations can design and steward ethical data governance systems that embody consent, transparency, and purpose. This trust infrastructure becomes foundational to how members, and broader stakeholders, engage.

Example: A peak body in education co-develops a member-owned data cooperative that aggregates learning outcomes while preserving privacy, enabling shared insight without commodification.

Evidence and Stewardship

Associations are often the only entities with the continuity, neutrality, and legitimacy to conduct sectoral benchmarking, horizon scanning, and longitudinal insight gathering. This evidence base informs not just practice, but public policy.

Example: A nutrition association curates a live, anonymised dashboard of dietary trends across demographic groups, feeding directly into preventive health policy formulation.

Adaptive Policy Capability

Perhaps most overlooked, associations act as feedback engines for government and regulators. They translate frontline experience into policy insight, surface unintended consequences, and propose practical adjustments based on lived implementation.

Example: A planning and infrastructure association convenes monthly "practice clinics" with state planners and local councils, identifying frictions in rollout and offering policy tweaks that speed up project approvals.

From ROI to Systemic Contribution

These three domains, economic, social, institutional, represent forms of value that defy traditional ROI calculations. They are not captured in quarterly revenue, website clicks, or event attendance. Yet they matter immensely to a healthy democracy, a capable workforce, and a coherent civil society.

Associations that embrace this broader vision of contribution are not just adapting to the times. They are shaping what comes next, with courage, clarity, and collective intent.

Metrics of Contribution: Designing a Value Dashboard

Boards should track mission-aligned value indicators such as:

Table 14-2 Mission-aligned value indicators

Value Area	Indicator Example
Ecosystem Impact	% of sector organisations using association-developed tools
Equity & Inclusion	Participation of under-represented groups in programs
System Learning	# of policy submissions informed by member insight
Collaboration Index	Avg. # of partners per strategic initiative
Public Trust	Stakeholder legitimacy index (perceptions, sentiment)

These indicators complement, but do not replace, financial reporting. They anchor purpose in real-world impact.

Funding Contribution: Beyond Dues and Grants

To deliver systemic value, associations may need new funding logics, including:

- **Outcome-based contracting** (e.g. pay-for-impact with public or philanthropic partners)
- **Cross-subsidy models** (e.g. commercial revenues funding open access resources)

- **Blended finance** (e.g. equity in social enterprises or joint platforms)
- **Platform partnerships** (e.g. co-investment in shared infrastructure with adjacent sectors)

The shift is from fee-for-service to value-for-impact. Associations must become impact entrepreneurs as much as advocates or facilitators.

Reframing the Annual Report: From Output to Contribution

Association reporting should reflect their *multi-sided platform logic*. A contribution-oriented report might include:

Table 14-3 Reporting for *multi-sided platform logic*

Report Section	Strategic Framing
Network Participation	Who is creating and sharing value?
Ecosystem Uplift	What capacity has been grown sector-wide?
Inclusive Reach	Who is benefiting, and who is missing?
Systemic Enablers	What infrastructure now exists because of us?
Future Signals	What capabilities are being built for tomorrow?

This approach builds trust, attracts new collaborators, and strengthens long-term legitimacy.

The Role of Boards in Stewarding Contribution

Boards must:

- Reaffirm purpose as a public good, not just a private benefit
- Embed contribution metrics in CEO KPIs and strategy dashboards
- Evaluate new initiatives not just for ROI, but for *ecosystem alignment*
- Review legacy programs through a contribution lens: *Does this still serve our system role?*

The Company Secretary can play a key role in ensuring that governance processes are aligned to impact tracking, not just financial reporting.

Case Insight: Systemic Value in Action

The Australian Council for International Development (ACFID) developed a sector-wide accountability framework, used by dozens of NGOs and referenced in government policy. Though not revenue-generating, it:

- Increased trust in the aid sector
- Reduced reputational risk across the ecosystem

- Provided infrastructure for future partnership with DFAT and the UN

This is systemic contribution, value that transcends any single program or budget line.

The End of Just Sustainable

Platform associations can, and should, be financially sustainable. But their true impact lies in making systems better: more ethical, more inclusive, more capable.

This is not a rhetorical shift, it is a governance one. The next generation of performance reporting, revenue strategy, and policy engagement must reflect this expanded role.

In the final part of this book, we introduce tools, templates, and applied models which consolidate the frameworks from earlier chapters into practical, board-ready assets.

Part V Tools, Templates, and Applied Case Models

Chapter 15. Analytical Toolkits for Strategic Decision-Making

From Strategy to Structure

Strategy is only as effective as the tools used to implement, monitor, and adjust it. In platform-based associations, where decisions affect multiple stakeholder groups, revenue streams, and interaction models, the analytical toolkits become governance infrastructure.

This chapter curates key tools introduced across the book, designed to help associations turn theory into boardroom practice. Each tool supports a specific decision context in terms of monetisation design, platform health, governance alignment, risk assessment, or contribution evaluation, and is structured for use in strategy sessions, CEO reports, or diagnostic workshops.

Monetisation Decision Matrix

Purpose: To evaluate and prioritise revenue model options based on strategic fit and implementation readiness.

Table 15-1 Monetisation Decision Matrix

Revenue Model	Strategic Fit	Member Acceptance	Complexity	Governance Risk	Priority
Tiered Membership	High	High	Medium	Low	✓
Data Benchmarking Sales	Medium	Low	High	Medium	×
Sponsored Webinar Series	High	Medium	Low	Medium	✓
Credentialing Spinout	High	Unknown	High	High	□

Use: Board/executive session on revenue innovation; pre-feasibility filtering.

Platform Pricing Readiness Index

Purpose: To assess whether an association is prepared to introduce or revise platform-aligned pricing models.

Table 15-2 Platform Pricing Readiness Index

Readiness Area	Current State	Rating (1–5)	Comments
Member Segmentation	Defined	4	Based on engagement levels
Value Proposition	Articulated	3	Needs testing with new segments
Infrastructure Support	Partial	2	CRM upgrades underway
Cultural Readiness	Mixed	3	Risk of perceived inequity

Use: Strategic planning workshop; fee strategy redesign.

Friction Audit Scorecard

Purpose: To identify where governance, operational, or relational friction is emerging in the system.

Table 15-3 Friction Audit Scorecard

Domain	Friction Type	Severity (1–5)	Example / Signal
Strategy	Structural	4	Overlapping committee mandates
Engagement	Relational	3	Member input not actioned
Operations	Procedural	5	4-week turnaround for approvals
Technology	Informational	2	Dashboard not aligned to KPIs

Use: Governance review; change-readiness assessment.

ROPI Calculator (Simplified Version)

Purpose: To assess platform investments not just by cost/benefit, but by ecosystem return.

Table 15-4 ROPI Calculator

Investment	Benefit Domain	Scope of Impact	Time to Return	ROPI Rating (1–5)
Member Portal Redesign	Engagement	High	6–12 months	4
Data Integration Layer	Infrastructure	Cross-org	18 months	5
Thought Leadership Series	Legitimacy/ Influence	Medium	Ongoing	3

Use: Strategic investment decision paper; infrastructure prioritisation.

Contribution Index Builder

Purpose: To measure platform value creation across users and partner types.

Table 15-5 Contribution Index Builder

Actor Group	Contribution Type	Frequency	Multiplier Effect	Index Value
Early-career Members	Content, feedback	High	Medium	3.5
Corporate Partners	Funding, data	Low	High	3.0
Educators	Content, curation	Medium	Medium	2.8
General Members	Participation	Low	Low	1.5

Use: Platform engagement dashboard; stakeholder value analysis.

Use of Tools: Boardroom and Executive Applications

Table 15-6 Tool Box Utilisation

Tool	Best Used By	Frequency	Decision Context
Monetisation Decision Matrix	Board + Exec	Annual	Diversifying revenue sources
Pricing Readiness Index	CEO + Strategy Lead	Mid-cycle	Updating membership models
Friction Audit Scorecard	Governance Committee	Pre-transformation	Identifying governance strain
Typology Alignment Tool	Board / Policy Lead	During strategy reset	Mapping governance gaps and reform opportunities
ROPI Calculator	Finance / CEO	Quarterly	Evaluating infrastructure and partnerships
Contribution Index Builder	Community / Comms	Ongoing	Value communication, investment in engagement

Infrastructure for Better Decisions

The future of association strategy will not be decided by instinct alone. These tools translate complexity into clarity, enabling boards and executives to govern with insight, align with value, and make trade-offs visible and deliberate.

In the next and chapter, we turn to live case applications of these tools and demonstrating how they've been used (or could be used) in real-world association scenarios.

Chapter 16. Applied Case Models and Illustrations

Learning by Application

Frameworks and diagnostics are only as powerful as the problems they help solve. This chapter brings the tools from earlier sections into applied focus through real and fictionalised cases. These are not only "success stories," but examples of how platform thinking, governance redesign, monetisation strategy, and contribution framing can shape actual association decisions.

Each case includes:

- A strategic problem or opportunity
- Tools or frameworks applied
- Outcomes, lessons, and strategic questions for boards

Case 1: PNA – Redesigning Membership and Monetisation

Context: The Professional Network Association (PNA) was losing younger members and revenue was flat. Its CPD was static and it had no digital engagement pathways beyond events.

Strategic Intervention:

- Used the **Platform Revenue Matrix** to introduce freemium digital access
- Adopted **Contribution Index Builder** to identify high-value engagement nodes
- Developed a new tiered membership model aligned with interaction levels

Outcomes:

- Reversed membership decline
- Revenue grew through upsells on peer-led mentoring and analytics dashboards
- Friction reduced by sunsetting legacy tiers and moving to real-time access models

Key Tool Highlighted: Pricing Readiness Index, Monetisation Matrix

Case 2: MTAA – Governance Friction in Technology Rollout

Context: The Medical Technology Association of Australia launched a digital standards library, but uptake lagged due to internal bottlenecks and unclear decision rights.

Strategic Intervention:

- Friction Audit Scorecard identified procedural and cultural drag
- Delegation framework updated using the **Governance Typology**
- Platform team empowered with agile feedback loops and stakeholder sandbox

Outcomes:

- Reduced cycle time for updates from 8 weeks to 2
- Increased platform engagement by 40% in the first year
- Board oversight shifted from operational sign-off to trust-based governance

Key Tool Highlighted: Governance Strain Index, Typology Alignment Tool

Case 3: Member-Led Innovation Portfolio

Context: To test new services but lacked innovation muscle and risk clarity.

Strategic Intervention:

- Introduced *Portfolio Thinking* to assess core vs transformational initiatives
- Board adopted an innovation fund with ringfenced budget
- Projects tracked through *ROPI metrics* and monthly learning loops

Outcomes:

- Three pilots sunset early, saving sunk costs
- One adjacent initiative, partner insights exchange scaled into new revenue

Culture shift: failure reframed as learning; risk welcomed, but bounded

Key Tool Highlighted: Portfolio Matrix, ROPI Calculator

Case 4: Systemic Contribution as Value Proposition

Context: As a regional innovation hub had strong community buy-in but limited monetisation. Board worried about sustainability without grant dependence.

Strategic Intervention:

- Reframed role from service provider to ecosystem enabler
- Introduced Systemic Contribution Dashboard as core board reporting tool
- Built monetisation around data insights and network access, not just space rental

Outcomes:

- Partner satisfaction increase as new collaboration metrics became visible
- Secure new multi-year private funding linked to ecosystem indicators
- Annual report structured around contribution domains (economic, social, institutional)

Key Tool Highlighted: Contribution Index, Systemic Value Metrics

Case 5: Aligning Platform Strategy with Public Legitimacy

Context: A peak body for disability services launch a digital inclusion platform, but uptake was slow among smaller providers and trust was low.

Strategic Intervention:

- Board applied *Trust & Legitimacy metrics* to diagnose member concern
- Community advisory panel formalised through G4–G6 governance zones
- Contribution-weighted access was reversed in favour of mission-based priority

Outcomes:

- Re-established legitimacy through procedural redesign and clearer social contract
- Broader participation unlocked new policy partnerships and philanthropic interest
- Friction converted into co-ownership and public engagement

Key Tool Highlighted: Governance Typology, Legitimacy Metrics

Table 16-1 Cross-Case Patterns

Strategic Lever	Common Result
Friction Audit + Delegation	Reduced governance drag; higher innovation responsiveness
Contribution Metrics	Better alignment between user value and resource allocation
Portfolio Thinking	Clearer investment signals; productive failure learning
Systemic Contribution Lens	New funding streams; stronger public narrative
Platform Revenue Mapping	Dues dependency replaced with multi-sided monetisation

Boardroom Questions for Reflection

1. What parts of our association still rely on linear, service-provider logic?
2. Where are our greatest sources of governance friction, and what does it cost?
3. How diverse is our revenue, and does it reflect our ecosystem role?
4. Are we measuring contribution or just consumption?
5. What would it take to redesign part of our work as a platform?

Practice Informs Precision

These case models demonstrate that platform thinking, applied with the right tools, can unlock not just transformation, but coherence, capacity, and impact. They also show that governance agility, economic framing, and systems strategy are no longer optional, they are the price of relevance.

In the final chapter, we turn from applied examples to a future-oriented synthesis: what associations must do next to evolve from 2.0 to 3.0 and play their full role in economic, civic, and platform ecosystems.

Chapter 17. Unlocking the Benefits of AI in Platform Associations

Capability, Use Cases, and Governance of AI as a Strategic Enabler

Artificial Intelligence (AI) is no longer an emerging technology, it is a general-purpose capability that underpins next-generation association platforms. For associations seeking to scale, personalise, and orchestrate dynamic ecosystems, AI enables strategic leaps in efficiency, insight, and member experience.

This annexure explores how AI can be embedded across core association functions. It provides practical guidance on implementation, governance, and ethical oversight, aligned with international standards such as *ISO 42001* and the *Australian AI Ethics Framework*. It is designed to help boards, CEOs, and strategy teams assess their AI readiness and govern its use responsibly.

Why AI Matters to Associations

AI is not a standalone tool. It acts as a force multiplier for:

- Member personalisation (e.g. content curation, CPD recommendations)
- Operational efficiency (e.g. workflow automation, chatbots)
- Insight generation (e.g. predictive analytics, engagement scoring)
- Governance augmentation (e.g. risk flagging, summarisation, fraud detection)

In platform associations, AI accelerates the shift from reactive service delivery to proactive orchestration.

AI Use Cases Across the Association Value Chain

Table 17-1 AI Use Cases

Function	AI Application	Strategic Benefit
Member Engagement	Personalised dashboards, smart recommendations, sentiment analysis	Higher retention and relevance
Learning & CPD	Adaptive learning, credential pathfinding, automated assessment	Competency-aligned progression
Customer Support	Chatbots, voice assistants, automated FAQs	Reduced staff burden, 24/7 support

Function	AI Application	Strategic Benefit
Operations	Document generation, approval flows, policy tagging	Lower friction, faster execution
Governance	Risk monitoring, board paper summarisation, decision traceability	Enhanced oversight and accountability
Analytics	Predictive churn models, cluster analysis, net value scoring	Data-driven decision-making

AI becomes most powerful when embedded into platform workflows, serving members and informing leaders in real time.

Strategic Opportunities and Capability Building

Associations can build AI capability by focusing on:

- **Data infrastructure**: High-quality, interoperable, privacy-compliant data
- **Integration**: Embedding AI tools into member services, CRM, and analytics platforms
- **Workforce development**: Training teams in AI literacy, prompting, and supervision
- **Strategic alignment**: Using AI to advance platform objectives, not just operational savings

Boards should treat AI as a *core capability domain*, alongside finance, governance, and digital maturity.

Governance and Ethical Risk Considerations

AI presents specific governance challenges. The table below outlines key risk domains and associated responsibilities.

Table 17-2 Governance and Ethical Risk Considerations

Risk Category	Governance Focus	Example Board Actions
Bias & Fairness	Monitor for discrimination or exclusion	Require auditability and bias testing
Transparency	Ensure AI use is visible and disclosed	Mandate flagging of AI-generated content
Privacy & Consent	Align with APP, GDPR, ISO 27701	Confirm lawful data sourcing and use

Risk Category	Governance Focus	Example Board Actions
Security	Protect models and inputs from misuse	Include AI systems in cyber risk registers
Accountability	Define roles across AI lifecycle	Adopt an AI Responsibility Matrix

Refer to ISO 42001 – AI Management Systems for system-level governance, and to the Australian AI Ethics Principles for values alignment.

Boardroom Tools: The AI Governance Register

Boards should require management to maintain an **AI Governance Register** capturing:

- What AI tools are in use and by whom
- Purpose, data sources, and outputs of each tool
- Oversight owner (e.g. product, IT, risk)
- Review cycle and performance measures
- Known risks, mitigations, and escalation protocols

This register supports transparency, accountability, and internal learning.

Implementation Roadmap for AI Adoption

Table 17-3 Implementation Roadmap for AI Adoption

Phase	Action	Outcome
Assess	Inventory current tools; identify high-potential use cases	Define scope and guardrails
Pilot	Test narrow AI tools with human-in-the-loop design	Build organisational trust and capability
Scale	Integrate AI into core systems; measure impact	Drive efficiency and personalised services
Govern	Establish policies, training, and reporting lines	Embed AI governance as part of digital strategy

Boards should request annual AI updates and integrate AI topics into risk and strategy committee agendas.

Boardroom Reflection Questions

- Where is AI already operating in our association, formally or informally?

- Are we clear on who is accountable for AI governance and ethics?
- Do we have member consent processes aligned with data-informed AI tools?
- How might AI shift our value proposition or competitive landscape?
- Are we training staff and boards in responsible AI use and oversight?

Conclusion

AI is not optional for platform-based associations, it is a foundational enabler of scalable, member-centred value. But without governance, AI becomes a risk multiplier rather than a strategic asset.

This annexure offers a roadmap for embedding AI responsibly. Associations that invest early in capability, transparency, and ethical design will be best placed to harness AI's full potential, while safeguarding trust and integrity.

Appendix A. AI Governance Register Template

This table is designed to track all AI tools, models, and systems in use across an association. It should be owned by the executive team but tabled regularly at the board or relevant committee (e.g. Technology, Risk, or Strategy).

Key Recommendations:

- Classify each tool by **decision impact** (informational / suggestive / automated).
- Flag tools where ethical risks exist and require oversight or human moderation.
- Assign a **named governance owner** for each tool.
- Review tools regularly for compliance, performance, and relevance.

Table 17-4 Monitoring Review Cycle

Review Cycle	Quarterly	Monthly	Bi-annual	Quarterly
Governance Owner	Head of Member Experience	Company Secretary	Director, Learning	Head of Insights
Ethical Risk (Y/N)	No	Yes (bias, hallucination)	Yes (exclusion bias)	Yes (profiling risk)
Human Oversight?	Yes	Yes	Partially	No
Decision Type	Suggestion	Informational	Recommendation	Predictive scoring
Input Data Sources	CRM records, FAQs	Board packs (PDF)	CPD history, member profile	Member engagement metrics
Business Unit	Member Services	Governance / CoSec	Education	Strategy & Insights
Purpose	Member service support	Board paper summarisation	Personalised learning pathways	Member retention forecasting
AI Tool / System	Chatbot (Zendesk AI)	GPT Summary Tool	CPD Recommender	Predictive Churn Model

Appendix B. Boardroom AI Capability Diagnostic

This quick-scan tool supports self-assessment by boards and executive teams across five core AI governance dimensions. Scores help identify where further investment or clarity is required.

Instructions: For each area, score your association from 1 (Not yet developed) to 5 (Well-developed and integrated). Use this for annual strategy sessions or transformation planning.

Table 17-5 AI Capability Diagnostic

Capability Area	Diagnostic Question	Score (1–5)	Board Follow-Up Action
1. Strategy Alignment	Is AI deployment clearly linked to strategic goals and member value creation?		
2. Governance Structures	Do we have defined oversight (e.g. committee, risk owner) for AI tools?		
3. Ethical Awareness	Are ethical principles (bias, transparency, fairness) applied to AI decisions?		
4. Capability and Literacy	Are board and executive teams trained in understanding AI risks and opportunities?		
5. Register and Inventory	Do we maintain an up-to-date register of all AI tools, use cases, and risks?		

Scoring Guide:

- **20–25**: High Capability – Strong AI governance culture; continue periodic review.
- **15–19**: Moderate – Address identified gaps in oversight, literacy, or ethics.
- **<15**: Low – Prioritise immediate action in risk mapping, training, and governance structures.

Chapter 18. Decision Toolkit for Transformation

Strategic Oversight, Risk Readiness, and Board-Level Action Planning

Platform transformation is not just an operational or technology shift, it is a governance challenge. It reconfigures decision rights, risk profiles, value flows, and stakeholder expectations. Boards must move beyond passive approval to active stewardship, ensuring strategic alignment, trust-based legitimacy, and oversight agility.

This annexure equips directors with four practical tools:

1. A Governance Readiness Matrix
2. A Digital Oversight Scorecard
3. A Platform Transformation Checklist
4. Boardroom Reflection Prompts

These tools help assess where an association stands, what risks it faces, and how governance structures can adapt to support platform-based innovation.

Governance Readiness Matrix

This matrix supports pre-decision assessments of platform initiatives, helping identify gaps across five key governance domains.

Table 18-1 Governance Readiness Matrix

Governance Area	Low Readiness (High Risk)	Moderate Readiness	High Readiness (Low Risk)	Board Action
Strategic Alignment	Digital seen as operational	Strategy exists but governance is patchy	Platform strategy fully board-aligned	Align with strategic plan, set KPIs
Stakeholder Engagement	No structured consultation	Ad hoc engagement	Embedded feedback loops	Establish formal engagement strategy
Revenue Diversification	Reliant on dues/events	Some new streams	Platform revenue is strategic pillar	Monitor monetisation oversight
Technology Risk Oversight	No AI/cyber review	Risks known but siloed	DGC and AI governance in place	Embed into board risk reporting

Governance Area	Low Readiness (High Risk)	Moderate Readiness	High Readiness (Low Risk)	Board Action
Decision Agility	Centralised, slow approvals	Partial delegation	Agile DOAs support change	Review DOA structure for speed and control

Digital Governance Oversight Scorecard

This board scorecard allows structured evaluation across eight areas of platform governance.

Table 18-2 Digital Governance Oversight Scorecard

Capability Area	Score (1–5)
Strategic alignment with transformation	
Board oversight of platform revenue model	
Cybersecurity and AI risk management	
Member and stakeholder engagement	
Digital literacy and director training	
Delegations of Authority for agile decisions	
Data ethics and privacy governance	
Performance monitoring and KPIs	

Scoring Key:

- **35–40**: Strong governance alignment
- **25–34**: Moderate – targeted improvements needed
- **<25**: High-risk posture – structural reform recommended

Platform Transformation Governance Checklist

Before launching a new platform initiative or digital investment, boards should confirm:

- The initiative aligns with our strategic goals and transformation roadmap
- A named board sponsor or committee is assigned oversight
- The project includes a stakeholder engagement plan
- Risks (technical, financial, ethical) have been identified and registered
- Intangible benefits (trust, brand, ESG) are part of the evaluation
- Delegations are in place to support rapid iteration with accountability
- AI, data, or automation systems have defined governance owners
- Scenario modelling (best/base/worst case) is available to the board

- Ongoing performance KPIs are agreed and reported

Use this checklist during business case approvals or digital strategy reviews.

Boardroom Reflection Prompts

To guide deeper conversations, boards may explore:

- Where are our governance structures enabling, or inhibiting, innovation?
- How do we balance agility with accountability in digital transformation?
- What assumptions are we making about member engagement and trust?
- Do our oversight mechanisms match the complexity of platform risks?
- Are we governing platform partnerships, data use, and AI tools with clear accountability?

These questions can form part of strategy retreats, committee planning sessions, or board evaluation cycles.

Conclusion

Governance is not a passive backdrop to digital change, it is an active enabler of responsible transformation. As associations move from service providers to ecosystem orchestrators, the governance model must evolve accordingly.

This toolkit provides the diagnostic clarity, strategic structure, and practical prompts needed to help boards lead with confidence in a platform-based future.

Governance Readiness Dashboard & Checklist

Table 18-3 Governance Readiness Dashboard & Checklist

Governance Area	Low Readiness (High Risk)	Moderate Readiness	High Readiness (Low Risk)	Board Action
Strategic Alignment	Digital seen as operational	Strategy exists but governance is patchy	Platform strategy fully board-aligned	Align with strategic plan, set KPIs
Stakeholder Engagement	No structured consultation	Ad hoc engagement	Embedded feedback loops	Establish formal engagement strategy
Revenue Diversification	Reliant on dues/events	Some new streams	Platform revenue is strategic pillar	Monitor monetisation oversight
Technology Risk Oversight	No AI/cyber review	Risks known but siloed	DGC and AI governance in place	Embed into board risk reporting
Decision Agility	Centralised, slow approvals	Partial delegation	Agile DOAs support change	Review DOA structure for

Governance Area	Low Readiness (High Risk)	Moderate Readiness	High Readiness (Low Risk)	Board Action
				speed and control

Table 18-4 Digital Governance Oversight Scorecard

Capability Area	Score (1–5)
Strategic alignment with transformation	
Board oversight of platform revenue model	
Cybersecurity and AI risk management	
Member and stakeholder engagement	
Digital literacy and director training	
Delegations of Authority for agile decisions	
Data ethics and privacy governance	
Performance monitoring and KPIs	

Table 18-5 Platform Transformation Governance Checklist

[ ] The initiative aligns with our strategic goals and transformation roadmap

[ ] A named board sponsor or committee is assigned oversight

[ ] The project includes a stakeholder engagement plan

[ ] Risks (technical, financial, ethical) have been identified and registered

[ ] Intangible benefits (trust, brand, ESG) are part of the evaluation

[ ] Delegations are in place to support rapid iteration with accountability

[ ] AI, data, or automation systems have defined governance owners

[ ] Scenario modelling (best/base/worst case) is available to the board

[ ] Ongoing performance KPIs are agreed and reported

Chapter 19. Business Model Canvas and Platform Application

Applying the BMC Framework to Design, Test, and Evolve Association Business Models

The Business Model Canvas (BMC), developed by Alexander Osterwalder and Yves Pigneur (2010), provides a strategic framework for assessing and refining business models. It is a powerful visual tool to design, test, and refine business models. Associations can use the BMC to align their value proposition, revenue streams, and engagement strategies in a structured and scalable manner.

For associations transitioning to platform-based models, the BMC helps identify opportunities for membership diversification, monetisation, and stakeholder collaboration. This annexure provides a step-by-step guide for applying the BMC to association business models.

This adapted Business Model Canvas supports associations in visually mapping, evaluating, and redesigning their business models. It provides a shared language for directors and executives to explore value creation, delivery, and capture across both traditional and platform-enabled association models.

Table 19-1 The Nine Components of the Business Model Canvas

Component	Description	Association-Specific Considerations
Value Proposition	The unique value an association provides to its members and stakeholders.	What makes the association indispensable? How does it differentiate itself from industry groups, free resources, or digital communities?
Member Segments	Defines the key groups the association serves.	Are members segmented by career stage, industry, location, or level of engagement? How do different member types derive value?
Key Activities	The essential functions required to deliver value.	What services, events, and programs define the association? (e.g., CPD, networking, advocacy, industry research).

Component	Description	Association-Specific Considerations
Key Resources	The assets and infrastructure needed to support activities.	What financial, human, and technological resources are critical to sustaining operations?
Revenue Streams	The ways the association generates income.	Beyond membership dues, are there transaction-based fees, sponsorships, CPD revenue, or licensing models?
Cost Structure	The primary expenses incurred in delivering value.	What are the fixed vs. variable costs? How can efficiency be improved while maintaining value?
Channels	The mediums used to deliver value and engage members.	Are digital platforms (e.g., online forums, apps, social media) optimised for accessibility and interaction?
Member & Stakeholder Relationships	The engagement and retention strategies.	What mechanisms drive continuous participation? How is personalisation and member loyalty fostered?
Key Partnerships	Collaborations that strengthen the association's value proposition.	Who are the strategic partners (e.g., industry sponsors, educational institutions, technology providers) that enhance offerings?

Using the BMC to Develop a Platform Business Model

Associations shifting to platform-driven models should adapt the BMC to focus on network effects, engagement loops, and monetisation diversification.

Mapping a Traditional Association vs. a Platform-Based Model

This adapted Business Model Canvas supports associations in visually mapping, evaluating, and redesigning their business models. It provides a shared language for directors and executives to explore value creation, delivery, and capture across both traditional and platform-enabled association models.

These examples illustrate the structural differences and evolving tensions between conventional service-delivery models and platform-based models focused on ecosystem enablement, network effects, and data-driven services.

Table 19-2 Traditional Association vs. a Platform-Based Model

Canvas Element	Traditional Association Example	Platform-Era Association Example
Key Partners	Sponsors, event venues, CPD providers	API developers, data providers, marketplace contributors
Key Activities	Membership renewals, event planning, advocacy	Platform moderation, data analytics, ecosystem orchestration
Value Proposition	Access to professional development and representation	Personalised learning, networked connections, co-created value
Customer Relationships	Email updates, helpdesk, conferences	Self-service dashboards, AI-guided interactions, peer forums
Customer Segments	Members by category or profession	Users, contributors, learners, partners
Key Resources	Staff expertise, venues, CRM	Platform infrastructure, data assets, algorithmic tools
Channels	Email, newsletters, events, website	Digital platforms, mobile apps, integration with member tools
Cost Structure	Salaries, venue hire, publishing	Cloud services, developer costs, platform scaling
Revenue Streams	Membership fees, CPD registration, advertising	Tiered access, data services, partner marketplaces

For associations looking to apply this framework in strategy workshops or governance sessions.

Steps for Associations to Apply the BMC

1. Define Value Proposition: Clarify the unique benefits offered to members.
2. Segment Membership: Identify distinct audience needs and tailor engagement strategies.
3. Assess Revenue Streams: Diversify beyond membership dues (e.g., pay-per-service, licensing).
4. Optimise Channels: Leverage digital platforms for continuous interaction.
5. Strengthen Partnerships: Develop alliances that align with industry trends and revenue opportunities.

Example: Applying the BMC

The Business Model Canvas provides a structured way to visualise and refine association revenue models. To see how this works in practice, we examine how the Australian Marketing Institute (AMI) successfully leveraged business model innovation to diversify revenue and enhance engagement.

Case Study: Australian Marketing Institute (AMI)

Transitioning to a Multi-Revenue Model

The Australian Marketing Institute (AMI) has successfully diversified its revenue model by integrating membership tiers, a professional job board, and corporate sponsorships into its platform-driven ecosystem. While it does not follow a freemium model, AMI has implemented a structured, value-based membership framework that offers tiered access to industry resources, career opportunities, and continuing professional development (CPD).

Key Adaptations:

Tiered Membership Model:

- AMI provides structured membership levels catering to different career stages, from students and early-career marketers to senior professionals.
- Members receive exclusive access to CPD programs, industry networking, and leadership opportunities.

Marketing Jobs Hub – A Professional Marketplace:

- AMI operates a job board where marketing professionals can access job listings, career advice, and employer connections.
- Employers pay to advertise premium job postings, creating a non-dues revenue stream.

Sponsorship & Corporate Partnerships:

- AMI collaborates with corporate partners who fund industry research, sponsored content, and networking events.
- Sponsors support industry awards, certification programs, and professional reports, ensuring ongoing industry engagement.

Key Impacts:

- **Increased Member Engagement**: By offering career services, professional recognition, and networking opportunities, AMI maintains strong retention and relevance.
- **Revenue Diversification**: Non-dues revenue from job board services, CPD programs, and sponsorships enhances financial resilience.
- **Industry Influence**: AMI strengthens its leadership in the Australian marketing sector by providing accredited learning pathways and professional certification programs.

Lessons for Other Associations:

- Monetisation should consider a align with professional value. By offering structured career pathways and premium services, AMI ensures that members see long-term benefits.
- A job marketplace can create recurring revenue. Industry-specific job boards provide financial sustainability while supporting member career growth.
- Sponsorships enhance engagement. By partnering with industry leaders, AMI maintains high-value sponsorship revenue while delivering resources and content to members.

AMI's multi-revenue strategy demonstrates how associations can go beyond traditional membership dues to create a self-sustaining, high-value ecosystem. While not a pure platform business model, its combination of membership tiers, career services, and sponsorships showcases a scalable, financially sustainable approach that other associations can replicate.

Applying the Business Model Canvas (BMC) – AMI Case Study

Table 19-3 Applying the Business Model Canvas

BMC Component	AMI Example	How to Apply This to Your Association
Value Proposition	AMI provides career growth, CPD programs, industry networking, and professional certification.	Define the unique benefits your association provides. What problem are you solving for members?
Member Segments	Early-career professionals, mid-career marketers, senior executives, and corporate partners.	Identify who your key audiences are. Do you serve students, professionals, businesses, or industry regulators?
Key Activities	Delivering CPD courses, professional certifications, networking events, and industry insights.	What are your core functions? (e.g., training, research, job boards, advocacy, accreditation).
Key Resources	Digital CPD platform, job board, sponsorship partnerships, industry accreditation programs.	List the essential assets needed for your association's success (platforms, technology, human resources, brand reputation).
Revenue Streams	Membership fees, job board fees, sponsored events, certification programs, corporate sponsorships.	Diversify your revenue sources: Which services or partnerships can be monetised? (e.g., pay-per-use training, sponsorships, industry research).

BMC Component	AMI Example	How to Apply This to Your Association
Cost Structure	Platform maintenance, content development, event organisation, marketing, staff salaries.	Identify your major expenses and optimise costs without reducing member value.
Channels	Website, CPD platform, social media, email marketing, industry partnerships.	Define how you communicate and deliver services to members (e.g., online learning, newsletters, virtual events).
Member & Stakeholder Relationships	Personalised career pathways, networking opportunities, leadership development programs.	How do you engage and retain members? (e.g., loyalty programs, mentorship, recognition awards).
Key Partnerships	Corporate sponsors, universities, marketing firms, event sponsors, CPD accreditation bodies.	Identify potential collaborators and sponsors that can help strengthen your association's value.

Designing a Platform-Driven Business Model

Using the AMI case study, an association can visualise how to transition from a traditional model to a platform-driven business model.

- Move Beyond Membership Fees – AMI diversified its revenue through CPD subscriptions, job board fees, and sponsorships. Associations should explore transaction-based income, marketplace facilitation, and industry partnerships.
- Leverage Network Effects – AMI facilitates professional networking and career services, ensuring continuous engagement beyond annual renewals. Associations should create ongoing interaction points through digital platforms.
- Adopt a Tiered Monetisation Model – AMI introduced structured membership tiers with premium benefits. Associations should explore freemium or tiered access models to attract diverse engagement levels.

Applying the BMC: A Step-by-Step Guide for Associations

1. Complete the Canvas – Use the template above to map out your current business model.
2. Identify Gaps – Look for missing opportunities (e.g., underutilised member engagement, untapped revenue sources).

3. Test New Models – Pilot different monetisation strategies (e.g., introducing paid job listings or launching sponsored webinars).
4. Scale and Optimise – Use data analytics to refine offerings, ensure financial sustainability, and enhance value delivery.

Boardroom Reflection Questions

- Have we mapped our current business model with all stakeholders included?
- Where do new revenue streams align with unmet member or partner needs?
- How are we managing the cost-to-value ratio across services?
- What platform enablers (e.g., matchmaking, co-creation) are we overlooking?
- Does our BMC reflect a scalable, diversified strategy, or a legacy structure?

Applying the Business Model Canvas (BMC) enables associations to transition from static membership models to dynamic, scalable platforms. The Business Model Canvas is not just a planning tool, it is a dynamic framework that allows associations to test, refine, and adapt their revenue strategies. By leveraging platform-driven business models, associations can expand their financial resilience while continuously delivering value to members and industry stakeholders.

Association Business Model Canvas Toolkit

Business Model Canvas Template (Association Version)

Use this template to map your association's current or future business model, with a focus on platform-based dynamics and value co-creation.

Table 19-4 Association Business Model Canvas Template

Key partners	Who enables value creation across the ecosystem?
Key activities	What core functions support delivery and interaction?
Value proposition	What unique value do we create or enable for members and stakeholders?
Customer (member) relationships	How do we engage different types of members and partners?
Customer segments	Who are our primary user groups, contributors, and stakeholders?
Key resources	What assets are required, people, technology, ip, data?

Channels	What touchpoints and platforms deliver engagement and services?
Cost structure	What are the major cost drivers? How does digital transformation change this?
Revenue streams	What income sources do we have or could we develop?
Platform opportunities	Where can we enable value exchange among users or third parties?

AMI Case Study: Platform-Based Association Model

Use this example as a benchmark or springboard for discussion.

Table 19-5 AMI Case Study: Platform-Based Association Model

Key Partners	Corporate sponsors, CPD providers, employers
Key Activities	CPD delivery, membership tiering, marketplace operations
Value Proposition	Career support, recognition, learning access
Customer Segments	Students, professionals, executives, industry partners
Customer Relationships	Structured membership tiers with increasing benefits
Channels	Website, CPD portal, job board, email
Key Resources	Digital platform, content library, partnerships
Cost Structure	Platform upkeep, marketing, staff
Revenue Streams	Membership dues, CPD income, job board fees, sponsorships

Part VI Economic Calculations

Chapter 20. Platform Economics and Value Logic

Understanding Cost Models, Network Effects, and Revenue Design in Association Platforms

This annexure provides a foundational economic lens through which to understand how modern associations create, scale, and sustain value using platform business models. It integrates theoretical principles, mathematical modelling, and applied strategy to help boards and executives make informed decisions on pricing, participation, monetisation, and structural design.

Platform economics is not an abstract theory, it is the core business logic of the digital economy. For associations, mastering this logic enables the shift from linear service delivery to ecosystem enablement. This annexure equips leaders with the concepts, comparative models, and design tools needed to unlock scalable, resilient, and multi-sided value.

The Economic Shift from Linear to Platform Models

Traditional associations operate under a linear model, value is produced by the association and consumed by members in exchange for dues. Revenue typically correlates with effort: more services, more cost. Scaling requires proportional increases in staff, time, or overhead.

Platform associations, by contrast, are value enablers. They facilitate peer-to-peer exchange, attract multiple participant groups (e.g. members, employers, sponsors), and monetise engagement, not just access. Their economics are defined by:

Table 20-1 Economic Shift from Linear to Platform

Platform Principle	Explanation
Network Effects	Value increases as more users engage, enhancing overall utility.
Lower Marginal Costs	Additional users can be served at near-zero incremental cost once infrastructure is in place.
Multi-Sided Revenue	Revenue comes from several actors, e.g., members, employers, advertisers, sponsors.
Data Monetisation	Behavioural and usage data can be transformed into insights and value-added products.

These characteristics yield scalable impact and financial resilience, particularly when paired with intelligent governance and data strategy.

Network Effects and Transaction Costs

Transaction Cost Theory and Value Efficiency

Platforms reduce the **costs of coordination and exchange** among users, which are traditionally borne by the association in a linear service model. These costs include:

Transaction Cost Analysis

Platforms reduce transaction costs, Tc, which can be represented as -

$$Tc = Sc + Nc + Ec$$

Where:

Sc - Search costs (e.g., finding providers or services).

Nc - Negotiation costs (e.g., agreeing on terms or contracts).

Ec - Enforcement costs (e.g., ensuring compliance with agreements).

Platforms minimise Tc by centralising information, automating workflows, and standardising processes. For example, in allied health, platforms reduce Sc by providing a directory of practitioners, Nc by offering pre-set service terms, and Ec by managing payments and compliance.

Platforms reduce costs by:

- Centralising information (e.g., course listings or practitioner profiles)
- Automating transactions (e.g., payment gateways, CPD certification)
- Embedding compliance into infrastructure (e.g., terms of use, data standards)

Table 20-2 Defining Network Effects

Network Effect Type	Definition	Example
Direct	More users on one side increase value for others on the same side.	More members = better networking and peer learning.
Indirect (Cross-Side)	More users on one side increase value for users on the other side.	More CPD providers attract more learners and vice versa.

These effects create positive feedback loops, driving exponential growth. However, they require active design, network effects are not automatic.

Positive vs. Negative Cross-Side Effects

Positive Effects: When more participants on one side increase the platform's value for the other side (e.g., more app developers attract more users to a software platform).

Negative Effects: When increased activity on one side diminishes value for the other side (e.g., excessive advertising on a platform could annoy users and drive them away).

Economics of Scale

Platforms aggregate costs across participants to generate economies of scale. The cost per user, Cu, decreases as the number of users increases -

$$Cu = \frac{Cf}{Qt} + Cv$$

Where:

Cf - Fixed costs (e.g., IT infrastructure).

Qt - Total number of participants on the platform.

Cv - Variable costs per user (e.g., customer support).

As Qt grows, Cu approaches Cv, driving cost efficiencies and increasing profitability.

Network Effects

Platforms benefit from *direct network effects*, where the value to participants increases with the number of other participants on the same side:

$$Ui = f(Qi)$$

Where Ui is the utility for a participant in group i, and Qi is the size of that group.

Indirect network effects arise when participation in one group enhances the utility of another group:

$$Ui = f(Qj), \qquad i \neq j$$

For instance, in allied health, an increase in practitioners (Qj) improves utility for patients (Ui). Or participants in one part of a platform, same CPP development, increases the number of members doping CPD. This is an example of a causal feedback loop:

- If CPD offerings grow in variety and relevance, engagement increases on the member side → which further attracts providers and sustains a virtuous cycle.
- This dynamic is the foundation of engagement loops and platform stickiness.

Clarifying Qj: It's Not Just Quantity That Matters

In basic network economics, the utility a user derives from a platform is often expressed as:

$$Ui = f(Qj), \qquad i \neq j$$

Where Qj is the number of participants on the other side of the platform. But in practice, this is a simplification. More advanced models recognise that:

- **Quantity without quality** may not increase value.
- **Match relevance** (e.g. finding the *right* mentor, CPD course, or job) is often more important than raw participant volume.
- **Elasticity**, how sensitive Ui is to changes in Qj can vary widely between groups.
- **Interaction matrices** (especially in complex ecosystems) are used to model how each group influences every other group, not just in pairs.

Boards and data leaders should ask:
Are we tracking participant growth, or *engagement quality* and *network fit*?

Platform Pricing and Cross-Side Network Effects

Pricing in multi-sided platforms is not about recovering cost, it is about optimising system-wide participation and enabling sustainable value exchange. For associations operating in a platform model, this means pricing must reflect the dynamic interactions between participant groups, often with intentional asymmetries.

Total Platform Value

Total value creation in a platform ecosystem can be expressed as:
The optimal price structure maximises total platform value (Vp) -

$$Vp = \sum_{i=0}^{n} PiQi - C$$

Where:

Pi Price charged to group i (e.g., users or providers).
Qi Quantity of group i participants.
C Total operating cost of the platform.

Platform pricing strategy is not about setting the right price per unit, it is about balancing multiple participation thresholds to maximise total ecosystem value.

Cross-Side Network Effects

Multi-sided platforms thrive on **cross-side interdependence**. An increase in users on one side often boosts the utility and growth of the other. This is captured by:

$$Nij = \frac{\partial Qi}{\partial Qj}$$

Where:

Nij represents how an increase in participants on one side (Qj) affects participation on the other side (Qi).

Nij Cross-side network effect between group i and j.

Ui Utility of participants on side i. (See below)

Qj Quantity of participants on side j.

If $Nij{>}0$, there is a positive cross-side effect; if $Nij{<}0$, there is a negative cross-side effect.

Cross-side network effects occur in multi-sided platforms when the value or utility of the platform for one group of participants increases due to the growth or participation of another group on the platform. This type of network effect is a defining characteristic of multi-sided platforms like marketplaces, social media platforms, and payment systems.

These dynamics are fundamental to understanding pricing leverage and value amplification.

Asymmetric Pricing Design

Platforms typically subsidise one group to attract another. Associations might:

- Offer free or low-cost access to **learners**, **members**, or **contributors**
- Charge **sponsors**, **employers**, or **premium partners** who extract greater value

This design depends on measurable cross-side feedback loops. The aim is not just revenue growth but maximising participation that multiplies ecosystem utility.

Platform-in-Practice Box: Cross-Side Network Effects in Practice

A mid-sized engineering association built a CPD platform open to both members and content providers. To accelerate growth, they offered free listing to vetted providers, which attracted high-quality content. This, in turn, increased member engagement, triggering a positive cross-side feedback loop. Eventually, premium placements and analytics became paid features, creating a sustainable revenue model aligned with ecosystem value creation.

Case in Point: Visa

In a two-sided platform, such as a payment system like Visa, there are typically two distinct user groups: merchants and cardholders.

Cross-side network effects are observed when an increase in cardholders (one side) makes the platform more valuable to merchants (the other side), and vice versa. More merchants accepting the card attracts more cardholders, creating a positive feedback loop.

Characteristics

1. **Interdependence**: The two (or more) sides of the platform are interdependent, meaning one side's participation directly affects the value perceived by the other side(s).
2. **Value Creation**: The platform's value is not solely from its features or offerings but also from the number and quality of participants across different sides.

Table 20-3 Platform Examples

Platform Type	One Side	Other Side
E-commerce Platforms (e.g., Amazon, eBay)	Buyers are more likely to join if there are many sellers offering products.	Sellers are attracted by a large base of buyers to sell to.
Ride-Sharing Platforms (e.g., Uber, Lyft)	Riders value the platform more when more drivers are available, reducing wait times.	Drivers value the platform more when there are more riders, increasing potential earnings.
Advertising-Supported Platforms (e.g., Facebook, YouTube)	Advertisers are attracted to platforms with a large number of users.	Users benefit (indirectly) from free access, funded by advertisers.

Visa's two-sided model illustrates this logic:

- **Cardholders** access the platform free or with rewards
- **Merchants** pay transaction fees
- Each group's growth reinforces the platform's utility for the other

Strategic Insights for Associations

- Not all growth is equal. Positive feedback loops are your strategic assets.
- Subsidies must be deliberate, if poorly aligned, they risk distorting network value.
- Boards should monitor not only user volume, but *who attracts whom* and *at what cost.*

Platform pricing often involves asymmetric models, where one group is subsidised while the other is monetised.

Measuring What Matters: Match Quality and Platform Value

In platform ecosystems, not all growth is equal. While network size is an important driver of value, the real source of utility lies in the relevance, quality, and effectiveness of interactions.

This insight reframes a key assumption of basic network economics. Where traditional models use:

$$Ui = f(Qi)$$

to express the utility a user on side *i* derives from the number of users on side *j*, this can be misleading in practice. High volumes of poorly matched, disengaged, or irrelevant users can erode trust and reduce perceived value.

To assess true value creation, platform associations should adopt match quality metrics, performance indicators that focus on the depth, relevance, and positive outcomes of interactions across the platform.

Key Match Quality Metrics and Their Formulas

Table 20-4 Key Metrics

Metric	What It Measures	Formula	Use Case
Interaction Density	Frequency of meaningful interactions per active user	$ID = \frac{T}{U_a}$	Are users finding value through connection?
Conversion Rate	Success rate of a specific interaction (e.g. view → enrolment)	$CR = \frac{C}{I} x\ 100\%$	Are people taking action after exposure?
Relevance Score	User-rated fit of content or matches (scaled 1–5)	$\overline{R} =$	Are offerings aligned with user needs?
Net Positive Engagement (NPE)	Ratio of positive to negative interactions	$NPE = \frac{P - N}{T}$	Is engagement enriching or eroding trust?

Definitions and Examples

Interaction Density (ID)

$$ID = \frac{T}{U_a}$$

T: Total interactions (e.g. messages, course starts, forum replies)
U_a: Active users during the period
→ **Higher ID** suggests a "sticky" platform where users actively participate.

Conversion Rate (CR)

$$CR = \frac{C}{I} \, x \, 100\%$$

C: Conversions (e.g. enrolments, completions)
I: Initial interactions (e.g. course views, email clicks)
→ Useful for testing **call-to-action strength**, platform usability, or pricing friction.

Relevance Score ($\bar{R}$)

$$\bar{R} = \frac{1}{n} \sum_{i=1}^{n} R_i$$

R_i: User-rated relevance (e.g. 1–5 stars)
n: Number of completed feedback responses
→ Helps refine search filters, recommendation engines, and segmentation logic.

Net Positive Engagement (NPE)

$$NPE = \frac{P - N}{T}$$

P: Positive interactions (likes, upvotes, positive reviews)
N: Negative signals (flags, complaints, dropouts)
T: Total interactions logged
→ A **sentiment-aware** engagement metric that highlights ecosystem health.

Why Match Quality Metrics Matter

These indicators:

- Detect **hidden performance risks** in large, underperforming networks
- Guide platform **design improvements** (e.g. onboarding, filtering, search)
- Justify **pricing tiers** or targeted engagement strategies
- Feed directly into **ROPI logic**, improving alignment with stakeholder value

Boardroom Insight

- High interaction volume is not the same as high platform value.
- Measure how well your ecosystem *works*, not just how big it is.

Measuring Utility of Participants

The utility of participants on side i in a multi-sided platform can be measured using quantitative and qualitative methods that capture how much value participants derive from the platform. While utility is inherently subjective, practical measures often rely on observable behaviours, survey data, and platform performance metrics.

Components of Utility

Utility Ui for participants on side i typically depends on:

Direct benefits: The core value provided by the platform (e.g., access to products, services, or users).

Network effects: The value derived from interactions with participants on the same or other sides.

Costs: Monetary or non-monetary costs incurred by participants.

The utility can be approximated as:

$$Ui = Vi + \sum_{j \neq i} Nij - Ci$$

Where:

Vi Value from direct benefits provided by the platform to side i.

Nij Cross-side network effect from side j to side i.

Ci Costs incurred by participants on side i.

Methods for Measuring Utility

At the core of members engagement is determining the value they achieve from using the "platform", be it accessing services offered or engaging with colleagues and other users.

Behavioural Data

Collecting and analysis of what members do is crucial.

Retention and Engagement Metrics:

- **Repeat Usage Rates**: High retention rates suggest participants find utility in continued platform usage.
- **Time Spent**: The time users spend on the platform indicates perceived value.
- **Frequency of Transactions**: For transactional platforms, higher transaction volumes suggest greater utility.
- **Churn Rates:** Lower churn rates (participants leaving the platform) imply higher perceived utility.

- **Conversion Rates**: For platforms facilitating transactions, the percentage of participants who complete desired actions (e.g., purchases, bookings) is a proxy for utility.

Financial Metrics

- **Willingness to Pay (WTP)**: Utility can be inferred from the maximum price participants on side iii are willing to pay for access or premium features on the platform.
- **Revenue per User (ARPU)**: Average Revenue Per User reflects the monetary value participants derive and their willingness to pay for services.
- **Subsidies or Discounts**: The amount required to attract participants to side iii indirectly measures their utility without subsidies.

Survey and Experimental Data

- **Surveys and Interviews**: Direct feedback on satisfaction, perceived value, and pain points offers insights into participant utility.
- Example questions:
  - "*How would you rate the value of [platform feature]?*"
  - "*How likely are you to recommend the platform?*"
- **Net Promoter Score (NPS)**: Measures participant satisfaction and loyalty by asking, "*How likely are you to recommend this platform to others?*"
- **Willingness to Accept (WTA) Compensation**: In experiments, participants can be asked how much they would need to be compensated to stop using the platform, providing an estimate of utility.

Platform-Specific Metrics

- **Match Quality**: On platforms where participants seek matches (e.g., job marketplaces, dating platforms), the success rate and quality of matches measure utility.
- Example: The percentage of successful hires on a job platform.
- **Interaction Density**: The number of meaningful interactions participants experience, such as messages sent or transactions completed.
- **Fulfilment Rate**: For supply-demand platforms (e.g., Uber), the percentage of requests fulfilled promptly is a measure of utility for users on both sides.

Challenges in Measuring Utility

- **Subjectivity**: Utility is inherently personal and may vary across users.

- **External Factors**: Utility measurements can be influenced by factors beyond the platform's control, such as economic conditions or competition.
- **Interdependencies**: Cross-side network effects can make it difficult to isolate utility for one side without considering the other sides.

Applications in Multi-Sided Platforms

For ride-sharing platforms (e.g., Uber): Utility for riders can be measured by average wait times, price satisfaction, and willingness to tip. The utility for drivers may be gauged through earnings, ride frequency, and satisfaction surveys.

For e-commerce platforms (e.g., Amazon): Buyer utility can be assessed through product variety, pricing, and fulfilment rates. The Seller's utility can be inferred from sales volumes, listing success rates, and platform fees.

By combining behavioural, financial, and experimental methods, platforms can effectively measure and optimise the utility of participants, ensuring sustainable growth and competitive advantage.

Table 20-5 Application of Utility models in Multi-Sided Platform

Section	Details
Key Considerations	
Alignment with Strategic Objectives	Assess alignment with long-term goals, competitive advantage, and mission. Enhance market positioning and stakeholder engagement.
Economic Benefits	Quantify increased revenues (e.g., sales growth, user base), cost savings (efficiencies, resource optimisation), and productivity improvements.
Intangible Gains	Include brand equity enhancement, stakeholder satisfaction, alignment with ESG goals, and regulatory compliance benefits.
Risk Assessment	Evaluate risks: ▪ Financial (e.g., cost overruns), ▪ Technological (e.g., obsolescence), and ▪ Market (e.g., adoption barriers). ▪ Member Satisfaction Identify and implement mitigation strategies.
Timeframe	Analyse short, medium, and long-term ROI. Recognise benefits like market share growth may accrue over time.

Financial Logic Model

Initial Investment Costs	Direct Costs: Platform development, hardware, software licenses, hosting, maintenance. Indirect Costs: Staff training, integration, opportunity costs.
Benefit Streams	Revenue Increases: New revenue sources (e.g., subscriptions, transactions). Cost Reductions: Automation, energy savings, resource optimisation. Risk Mitigation: Reduced compliance costs.
Calculation Model	Formula: $ROI(\%) = Net\ Benfits\ \frac{(Total\ Gains - Total\ Costs)}{Total\ Costs} x\ 100$ Sensitivity analyses: Vary assumptions for uncertainties (e.g., growth rates).
Break-even Analysis	Identify the point where cumulative benefits offset total costs. Define timelines for achieving break-even under different scenarios.
Scenario Modelling	Best Case: Optimal adoption, full cost efficiencies. Base Case: Most likely outcome based on industry trends. Worst Case: Delays, cost overruns, slow adoption. Consider using dynamic modelling tools.
Sustainability Metrics	Quantify ESG-related impacts: energy savings, societal benefits (e.g., community engagement), alignment with circular economy principles.
Visual Representation	Dashboards and Charts: ▪ Payback Period: Time to recover investments. ▪ Net Present Value (NPV): Total value of future net benefits. ▪ Internal Rate of Return (IRR): Return rate for break-even.

Implementation Roadmap

Phase 1: Feasibility Analysis	Conduct market viability and platform readiness assessments.
Phase 2: Development & Deployment	Allocate resources, establish timelines, and execute platform rollout.
Phase 3: Performance Monitoring	Track KPIs: adoption rates, revenue growth, and cost savings.

Governance Implications

Platform models increase complexity and governance responsibility. Boards must account for:

- Cross-side value trade-offs
- Data governance and privacy
- Digital and ethical risk management
- Pricing fairness and cannibalisation risk
- Revenue-model oversight

Use agile governance tools (e.g. Digital Governance Committees, ISO 37000, ISO 42001) to align oversight with economic design.

Boardroom Reflection Questions

- Are we pricing in alignment with network dynamics and user utility?
- Do we understand our cost structure per user segment?
- How diversified are our revenue flows, can we withstand external shocks?
- What cross-side incentives are we using, and are they working?
- Are our governance structures fit for multi-sided, data-driven models?

Part 5: Financial Logic and ROI Models

Applied Revenue Models in Associations

Table 20-6 Applied Revenue Models in Associations

Model	Description	Example Applications
Freemium	Free access with paid upgrades	Forums, analytics tools, digital CPD
Transaction Fees	Commission on platform activity	CPD bookings, job listings
Subscriptions	Recurring payments for access	Learning libraries, credential platforms
Sponsorship	Brands pay for access and visibility	Webinars, insight reports
Data Monetisation	Anonymised data products	Workforce trend reports, benchmarking dashboards

These models create dynamic revenue streams untethered from headcount or event attendance.

Table 20-7 Five-Level Framework for Pricing Models

Level	Approach	Characteristics	Limitations	Features of Improved Pricing Strategy
1. Inadequate	Flat Pricing	- Single-tier or uniform pricing.	- Overcharges or	- Begin segmentation by user needs.

Level	Approach	Characteristics	Limitations	Features of Improved Pricing Strategy
		- No differentiation across user segments. - No consideration of costs or market demand.	undercharges certain user groups. - Misses revenue opportunities. - Prone to user dissatisfaction.	- Consider cost and basic demand trends.
2. Basic	Simple Tiered Pricing	- Introduces 2–3 tiers (e.g., Basic, Standard, Premium). - Based on static assumptions about user preferences.	- Limited data to refine tiers. - Ignores elasticity of demand. - Lacks flexibility for market changes.	- Add simple metrics like Cost per User (Cu) and willingness to pay analysis.
3. Intermediate	Dynamic Tiered Pricing	- Utilises user data to refine tiers and features. - Pricing adjusts based on demand or competitor benchmarks.	- Requires manual adjustments. - Limited ability to test pricing dynamically across groups.	- Incorporate A/B testing for pricing. - Include cross-side network effects in tier design.
4. Advanced	Data-Driven Tiered Pricing	- Combines historical data and demand elasticity models. - Factors in variable costs and segment-specific willingness to pay.	- Higher operational complexity. - May require external data integration tools (e.g., BI platforms).	- Automate tier adjustments based on real-time analytics. - Expand segmentation to micro-targeting.
5. Robust	Predictive Pricing Models	- Uses AI and machine learning for real-time price optimisation. - Incorporates user behaviour, competition,	- Requires significant investment in technology and expertise. - Potential for over-reliance on algorithms.	- Continuously refine pricing based on user behaviour trends and predictive market changes.

Level	Approach	Characteristics	Limitations	Features of Improved Pricing Strategy
		and external economic factors.		

Dynamic Pricing in Platform-Based Associations

As associations evolve into digital platforms, pricing moves from static tiers to adaptive, data-informed models. Dynamic pricing enables organisations to respond in real time to user behaviour, demand fluctuations, willingness to pay, and market conditions, unlocking both revenue optimisation and personalisation.

What Is Dynamic Pricing?

Dynamic pricing refers to *adjusting prices in real time or near-real time* based on one or more variables:

- User behaviour and engagement
- Time of day or registration window
- Inventory availability or event capacity
- Segment-based value perception
- Cross-side network activity (e.g. demand–supply balance)

Examples for Associations

Table 20-8

Application	Dynamic Variable	Example
CPD enrolments	Time-based	Early bird vs last-minute pricing
Membership tiers	Engagement-driven	Discounts for high-referral or highly engaged users
Job board listings	Demand elasticity	Premium pricing during peak hiring periods
Events or webinars	Supply/demand	Lower pricing as seats fill to boost balance

Implementing Dynamic Pricing Responsibly

Table 20-9

Step	Key Action	Strategic Rationale
1. Segmentation	Identify distinct user segments by behaviour or value	Aligns price with perceived benefit

Step	Key Action	Strategic Rationale
2. Elasticity Testing	Conduct A/B tests on price sensitivity	Empirically determine WTP
3. Trigger Rules	Define logic (e.g. time, behaviour, demand) for adjustment	Ensures transparency and predictability
4. Automation Layer	Use pricing engines or AI tools for deployment	Reduces admin cost, increases agility
5. Oversight and Fairness	Introduce governance review points	Avoids perception of price discrimination or unfairness

Governance and Ethical Considerations

- Transparency: Communicate clearly when prices may vary
- Fairness: Avoid penalising low-income, low-engagement, or marginalised segments
- Data ethics: Ensure input data is accurate, unbiased, and consented
- Appeals or guarantees: Consider price guarantees, refund windows, or "best value" pledges to build trust

Reflection Questions for Boards

- Are we using pricing as a static label, or as a strategic engagement tool?
- What user behaviours could we reward through pricing flexibility?
- Do we have governance protocols for real-time pricing changes?
- How do we ensure fairness and trust in segmented or AI-assisted pricing?

Case Study: CPD Pricing Strategy

Comparing Static vs Dynamic Pricing Models

Background

The association operates a national CPD platform. Its goals include increasing member participation, generating non-dues revenue, and engaging more diverse member segments across different career stages.

Historically, AHA used a flat-rate pricing model for all CPD courses:

- Fixed price: $220 per course
- No variation for demand, time of enrolment, or member type
- Discounts limited to infrequent seasonal promotions

In FY2023, participation plateaued. Member surveys indicated the model was inflexible, particularly for early-career professionals and students.

Phase 1: Static Pricing Model

Performance Outcomes (FY2023)

- Course price: $220 (uniform)
- Courses sold: 1,800
- Total revenue: $396,000
- Conversion rate (page views to enrolments): 8%
- Enrolments in high-demand courses: 85 per course
- Enrolments in low-demand courses: 23 per course
- Cart abandonment rate: 35%
- Complaints about affordability: Frequent (especially from early-career members)

Challenges Identified

- Poor engagement among budget-constrained members
- Over-reliance on one-size-fits-all pricing
- Inefficient course utilisation due to inability to adjust price based on demand

Phase 2: Dynamic Pricing Model (Pilot FY2024)

- The association introduces a rule-based dynamic pricing to test more responsive approaches:
  - Early-bird discount: 20% off for enrolments more than four weeks in advance
  - Capacity pricing: 10% increase when enrolment hits 75% capacity
  - Engagement reward: 15% discount for members completing three or more courses in the last six months
  - Equity adjustment: 5% premium for employer-paid enrolments, 10% discount for student members

Performance Outcomes (FY2024 Pilot)

- Average course price: $207 (range from $165 to $250)
- Courses sold: 2,400
- Total revenue: $496,800
- Conversion rate: 11.5%
- Enrolments in high-demand courses: 110 per course
- Enrolments in low-demand courses: 42 per course
- Cart abandonment rate: 19%
- Member complaints: Significantly reduced

Table 20-10 Pricing approach comparative summary

Dimension	Static Pricing	Dynamic Pricing	Insight
Revenue	$396,000	$496,800	Increased revenue through pricing flexibility
Accessibility	Uniform pricing	Tiered, needs-based	Improved access for students and early-career members
Conversion Rate	8%	11.5%	Greater confidence to purchase due to perceived fairness
Course Utilisation	Unbalanced	Demand-optimised	Smoothed enrolments across all courses
Member Satisfaction	Mixed	High	Fewer complaints and higher ratings
Admin Complexity	Low (manual)	Moderate (automated rules)	Required setup but manageable with existing systems

Strategic Implications

- AHA moved from pricing for simplicity to pricing for engagement and value.
- Pricing strategy now supports equity, participation, and revenue goals simultaneously.
- Rule-based automation allowed responsive pricing without loss of governance control.
- Pricing insights also informed marketing, course design, and member segmentation strategies.

Boardroom Reflection Questions

- Could we use pricing as a tool for participation, not just income?
- Where in our current offerings would dynamic pricing make the biggest difference?
- Do we have enough data to segment and price responsibly?
- What governance safeguards are needed to manage trust, fairness, and transparency?

Chapter 21. Return on Platform Investment (ROPI) Evaluation

Measuring Financial and Ecosystem Returns on Digital and Strategic Initiatives

This annexure equips boards, CFOs, and executive leaders with a comprehensive framework to evaluate the viability, performance, and ecosystem impact of strategic initiatives, particularly those involving platform infrastructure, digital transformation, or multi-stakeholder engagement.

Profit Maximisation and Multi-Sided Value Capture

Platforms aim to maximise profit (π)

$$\pi = \sum_{i}^{n} PiQi - \left(Cf + \sum_{i}^{n} CiQi \right)$$

Where:

Ci - Marginal cost per participant in group i.

Profit maximisation balances subsidising one group (e.g., patients in allied health) while charging the other (e.g., providers).

Optimal platform economics often involve:

- Subsidising low-monetisation segments to build scale (e.g. free member tools)
- Charging high-value segments that extract premium value (e.g. sponsors, employers)

Customer Lifetime Value

Customer Lifetime Value (CLV) estimates the net financial value a member or user generates over their expected time on the platform. For associations, it helps guide investment in recruitment, onboarding, and retention strategies.

A discounted CLV model:

$$CLV = \frac{R \times L}{1 + r} - Ca$$

Where:

R - Average revenue per period.

L - Expected lifetime of the participant on the platform.

r - Discount rate.

Ca - Cost of acquiring the participant.

Alternately, platform associations optimise CLV by:

- Increasing retention (extending L) through engagement and personalisation
- Growing average revenue per member (R) through value-added services
- Reducing acquisition cost (Ca) via referrals, partnerships, or freemium-to-premium conversions.

$$CLV = \sum_{t-1}^{L} \frac{R_t}{(1+r)^t} - C_a$$

Where:

R_t: Revenue from customer in time period t

$L: Customer\ lifetime\ (in\ periods)$

r: Discount rate

C_a: Customer acquisition cost

This reflects Net Present Value (NPV) of future revenue streams minus acquisition costs.

Platforms invest heavily in reducing Ca while maximising L through engagement and retention strategies.

This is particularly relevant when developing strategies for recruitment of members and evaluating what the lifetime value will be.

Cost per Acquisition (CPA)

CPA is a key metric for evaluating the efficiency of user acquisition

$$CPA = \frac{M}{Qa}$$

Where:

M - Marketing expenditure.

Qa - Number of participants acquired.

Limits of Traditional ROI Methods

While traditional ROI tools remain useful, they fall short in capturing the full value profile of platform-based investments. The *ROPI framework* introduced here extends standard metrics to account for network effects, alignment risk, and strategic ecosystem dependencies. Together, these tools help decision-makers assess not only whether an investment will pay off, but *why*, *how*, and *for whom*.

Foundational Logic: What Makes Platform Investment Different?

- Value is co-created, not delivered
- Gains are distributed and often intangible
- Risk is structural (co-innovation, adoption, sequencing)
- Outcome depends on alignment, not just inputs

Platform economics demands we evaluate not just returns, but the configuration of contributors who enable them.

Traditional Tools Still Matter: Core ROI Metrics

Introduce and define standard tools, these remain essential but are only part of the picture.

Table 21-1 Core ROI Metrics

Metric	Definition	Use Case
ROI (%)	Return on financial input	High-level financial viability
NPV	Future net gains discounted to present	Long-horizon planning
IRR	Break-even discount rate	Investment comparisons
Payback Period	Time to recover costs	Liquidity considerations
Break-even Point	Users needed to recover fixed cost	Scalability threshold

Linear Model ROI Formula

$$ROI(\%) = \frac{(Total\ Gains - Total\ Costs)}{Total\ Costs} x\ 100$$

Alternatively,

$$ROI = \frac{\pi}{I}$$

Where:

π = Profit $(Total\ Gains - Total\ Costs)$

I - Total investment in platform development and operations.

High ROI is achieved by leveraging network effects and minimising Cu (cost per user).

Key Considerations for ROI Assessment

A thorough ROI analysis requires evaluating multiple dimensions beyond direct financial returns. The table below outlines key considerations:

This Annexure provides a structured framework for conducting an ROI analysis tailored to platform-based business models. It is designed to assist governing bodies in making informed decisions that align with legal obligations and strategic objectives.

Table 21-2 Key Considerations

Component	Description
Alignment with Strategic Objectives	Assess alignment with long-term goals, competitive advantage, and mission. Enhance market positioning and stakeholder engagement.
Economic Benefits	Quantify increased revenues (e.g., sales growth, user base), cost savings (efficiencies, resource optimisation), and productivity improvements.
Intangible Gains	Include brand equity enhancement, stakeholder satisfaction, alignment with ESG goals, and regulatory compliance benefits.
Risk Assessment	Evaluate risks: Financial (e.g., cost overruns), Technological (e.g., obsolescence), and Market (e.g., adoption barriers). Member Satisfaction Identify and implement mitigation strategies.
Timeframe	Analyse short, medium, and long-term ROI. Recognise benefits like market share growth may accrue over time.

Where this formula *assumes* clear cost attribution and benefit capture, in platform environments, the underlying assumptions don't hold, particularly where:

- Value is co-created across actors.
- Gains may be intangible or realised over long time horizons.
- Ecosystem misalignment can undermine even well-funded initiatives.

Boards must therefore expand their financial lens to capture *networked value*, *risk-adjusted outcomes*, and *ecosystem readiness*.

Core Evaluation Metrics

Table 21-3

Metric	Definition	Use Case
Net Present Value (NPV)	Value of future net gains discounted to today	Long-term investment analysis
Internal Rate of Return (IRR)	Discount rate where NPV = 0	Comparing competing investment options
Payback Period	Time to recoup investment	Short-term viability and liquidity impact
Break-Even Point	Users or volume needed to recover fixed costs	Platform scaling thresholds

Break-Even Analysis and Scenario Modelling

Table 21-4

Model Type	Key Question
Best Case	What if adoption exceeds expectations and costs are minimal?
Base Case	What is the most likely outcome given current assumptions?
Worst Case	What if uptake is low or unexpected costs emerge?

A. Break-Even Analysis

Platforms must reach a critical mass of participants to achieve profitability

$$Qt = \frac{Cf}{Pi - Ci}$$

Where:

Q_t = number of users needed to break even

C_f = fixed costs

P_i = price per user

Ci = cost per user

The break-even point is lower for platforms with significant economies of scale.

Application of Economic Models

1. **Transaction Cost Reduction** - Platforms significantly reduce Tc, particularly in fragmented markets like allied health. Shared tools (e.g., scheduling systems and EHRs) reduce administrative costs while enabling efficient provider-patient matching.

2. **Asymmetric Pricing Models** - Platforms often subsidise patients (free consultations, discounts) while charging providers (subscription fees, pay-per-use models) to maximise Vp.
3. **Cost Aggregation and Collaboration** - By aggregating infrastructure costs, platforms enable providers to access advanced tools (e.g., telehealth systems) at a fraction of standalone costs. This cost-sharing mechanism fosters collaboration and scales services effectively.
4. **Network Effects in Practice** – For associations with platform business model, indirect network effects emerge when more members/users join, attracting more members and/or users. These effects enhance platform value exponentially as participation grows.

ROPI: Return on Platform Investment

As associations evolve into platform-based ecosystems, traditional ROI metrics fall short. Standard input–output logic fails to capture co-creation, ecosystem friction, and intangible value.

ROPI reframes investment performance through the lens of ecosystem alignment and participation dynamics. Inspired by Adner's (2016) ecosystem-as-structure framework, ROPI highlights the strategic risk posed by misaligned roles, timing, or incentives across partners and users. This gives rise to two ROPI perspectives:

A structural definition:

A conceptual Model useful for strategic reflection and alignment planning:

ROPI = Projected Platform Value – Value Lost to Ecosystem Misalignment

A quantitative ratio:

Applied for performance tracking, dashboard reporting, and capital review cycles.

$$ROPI = \frac{Net\ Benefits\ (Gains - Costs)}{Total\ Costs}\ x\ 100$$

Where traditional ROI is input-output focused, ROPI incorporates structural risk, such as:

- **Co-innovation risk** (can partners deliver?)
- **Adoption chain risk** (will they engage?)
- **Timing risk** (are roles sequenced correctly?)

Boards and CFOs can apply ROPI thinking using structural metrics like:

- Partner activation rate
- Time-to-value from integration

- Friction in onboarding or service delivery
- Ecosystem "drop-off" points

By embedding ecosystem alignment into investment evaluations, associations gain a more holistic view of performance, enabling smarter capital allocation, strategic sequencing, and risk mitigation in platform environments.

Platform-in-Practice: Applying ROPI to a Member Mentoring Platform

Scenario

An association invests $180,000 in a new peer-to-peer mentoring platform to boost early-career engagement. The business case forecasts a three-year revenue uplift of $240,000 through increased member retention and CPD purchases.

Traditional ROI Evaluation

$$ROI = \frac{\$240{,}000 - \$180{,}000)}{\$180{,}000}\ x\ 100 = 33.3\%$$

This appears financially sound.

However, rollout metrics reveal structural issues:

Partner institutions were slow to promote the program.

60 percent of new users abandoned the onboarding process before completing mentor profiles.

Corporate partners delayed engagement campaigns, missing the graduate recruitment cycle.

ROPI in Action

Instead of evaluating only inputs and outputs, the association applies a Return on Platform Investment (ROPI) lens to assess structural alignment and ecosystem performance:

Table 21-5 Underperformance measures

Structural Risk	Observation	Metric
Co-innovation Risk	University and employer partners missed rollout windows	Partner Activation Rate: 45%
Adoption Chain Risk	Mentees failed to complete onboarding	Onboarding Drop-Off: 60%
Timing Risk	Program launched after peak demand from graduating members	Time-to-Value: 5-month lag

ROPI Insight

Despite a positive ROI, ecosystem misalignment eroded actual value delivery:

- Engagement dropped due to poor sequencing.
- Friction in onboarding reduced user trust.
- Delayed partnerships reduced perceived credibility.

Strategic Response

- Using ROPI indicators, the board and executive team recalibrated:
- Mapped the adoption chain to synchronise onboarding, marketing, and platform readiness.
- Introduced a co-contribution model to increase partner accountability and early buy-in.

Added *ROPI structural metrics* to board reporting, including: Partner activation rate; Drop-off index across the onboarding journey; and First 60-day engagement velocity

Adjusted ROPI Calculation

Now apply the structural correction factor to account for ecosystem misalignment. We'll estimate the value erosion based on:

Table 21-6 Adjusted ROPI Calculation

Structural Factor	Indicator	Estimated Value Erosion
Partner Activation	Only 45% engaged as planned	−15%
Onboarding Drop-Off	60% failed onboarding	−25%
Delayed Value Realisation	5-month time lag in ecosystem uptake	−10%
Total ecosystem misalignment penalty		-50%

Adjusted Value Realised: $\$240{,}000 \times (1 - 0.50) = \$120{,}000$

Now recalculate ROPI:

$$ROI = \frac{(\$240{,}000\ x\ 50\%) - \$180{,}000)}{\$180{,}000}\ x\ 100 = -33.3\%$$

Interpretation

- Traditional ROI suggests a healthy project with +33.3% return.
- ROPI, factoring in structural misalignment, reveals a negative return of -33.3%.

Takeaway

ROPI made visible what traditional ROI could not: friction, misalignment, and strategic sequencing risks. By diagnosing these factors early, the association not only improved platform performance but also strengthened long-term trust, value flow, and economic coherence.

Strategic Response

Adjusted ROPI Calculation

Interpretation

Structural Metrics for ROPI Assessment

Table 21-7 Structural Metrics for ROPI Assessment

ROPI Factor	Indicator	Strategic Question
Partner Activation	% of partners onboarded on time	Are enablers engaged and ready?
Adoption Velocity	Time-to-value post-launch	How quickly is value realised?
Friction Points	Drop-off in onboarding or engagement	Where does the value chain weaken?
Ecosystem Alignment	Degree of interdependence clarity	Are roles and incentives understood?

Boards can use these metrics in investment approvals, post-implementation reviews, and portfolio monitoring.

Worked Example: Scoring-Based Structural ROPI Formula

We assign *weights* to each of the four ROPI structural metrics based on strategic importance, and then compute a **ROPI Adjustment Factor (RAF)** to scale the financial ROI.

Step 1: Define the ROPI Structural Formula

$ROPI_{adjusted} = ROI \times RAF$

Where:

$$RAF = (W1 \cdot S1) + (W2 \cdot S2) + (W3 \cdot S3) + (W4 \cdot S4)$$

W_n = Weight for each factor (sum to 1)
S_n = Scaled score (0 to 1) for each factor:
1 = Fully aligned
0.5 = Partially aligned
0 = Misaligned

Step 2: Apply Scores and Weights

Table 21-8

Metric	Score (Sn)	Weight (Wn)	Weighted Score
Partner Activation (% onboarded)	0.5	0.25	0.125
Adoption Velocity (Time-to-value)	0.75	0.25	0.1875
Friction Points (Drop-off rate)	0.4	0.25	0.10
Ecosystem Alignment (Role clarity)	0.6	0.25	0.15
Total RAF			0.5625

Step 3: Apply RAF to ROI

If Traditional ROI = 40%, then:

$$ROPI_{adjusted} = 40\% \times 0.5625 = 22.5\%$$

Interpretation

This example shows that although the ROI looked strong at **40%**, structural issues in the platform ecosystem reduced the **effective return** to **22.5%**. This highlights risks that might otherwise go unnoticed in traditional evaluation methods.

Table 21-9 ROPI Calculation

ROPI Structural Metric	Score (0–1)	Weight	Weighted Score
Partner Activation	0.5	0.25	0.125
Adoption Velocity	0.75	0.25	0.1875
Friction Points	0.4	0.25	0.10
Ecosystem Alignment	0.6	0.25	0.15
Total RAF			0.5625
Adjusted ROPI (ROI × RAF)			22.5%

Integrating Intangible Value into ROI Logic

Modern performance metrics should include:

Table 21-10 Integrating Intangible Value into ROI Logic

Intangible Gain	Example
Brand Equity	Visibility, reputation, thought leadership
Member Trust	Transparency, data governance, ethical design
Social Impact	Access, equity, ESG alignment
Innovation Capability	Experimentation capacity, platform agility

Assign *qualitative ratings* or *proxy measures* (e.g. Net Promoter Score, engagement rates) to embed these in ROI evaluations.

Scenario Modelling for Platform Investment

Table 21-11 Scenario Modelling for Platform Investment

Scenario Type	Description	Use
Base Case	Expected outcomes based on current data	Primary planning input
Best Case	High adoption, low cost	Stress test for upside potential
Worst Case	Delays, disengagement, cost blowouts	Risk containment planning

Tools such as Monte Carlo simulation, probabilistic forecasting, or traffic-light scenario maps can support more nuanced board decisions.

Governance and Accountability for ROI/ROPI

To ensure transparent decision-making, governing bodies should integrate ROI assessments into board governance cycles.

Table 21-12 Governance Best Practice

Governance Best Practice	Implementation Approach
Board Oversight of ROI Metrics	Ensure ROI analysis is reviewed quarterly at governance meetings.
Risk-Based Decision-Making	Align financial, technological, and member adoption risks with governance frameworks.
Stakeholder Engagement	Include member feedback loops in investment decisions to assess perceived platform value.
Regulatory & Compliance Alignment	Ensure ROI models incorporate legal, ethical, and industry-specific compliance standards.

Boards should embed financial evaluation into governance cycles via:

- Quarterly ROI/ROPI tracking dashboards
- Clear delegation thresholds for capital allocation
- Board-level project sponsors with oversight responsibility
- Integration into the Digital or Strategy Committee charter

This ensures investment performance is not only approved, but *actively stewarded.*

Implementation Roadmap

Table 21-13 Implementation Roadmap

Component		Description
Phase 1:	Feasibility Analysis	Conduct market viability and platform readiness assessments.
Phase 2:	Development & Deployment	Allocate resources, establish timelines, and execute platform rollout.
Phase 3:	Performance Monitoring	Track KPIs: adoption rates, revenue growth, and cost savings.

Capital Value: Valuing the Platform as a Strategic Asset

While Return on Investment (ROI) and Return on Platform Investment (ROPI) provide critical tools to assess performance and alignment, they do not fully account for the long-term strategic value of the platform itself. Capital value refers to the economic and strategic worth of the platform infrastructure, data assets, user base, and ecosystem positioning. It shifts the board's perspective from cost-benefit logic to asset stewardship and future potential.

Valuation Approaches for Platform-Based Associations

1. Discounted Cash Flow (DCF) Valuation:

This method estimates the present value of expected future free cash flows:

$$Value = \sum \frac{FCT_t}{(1+r)^t}$$

Where:

FCT_t: Projected free cash flow in year t

r: Discount rate reflecting platform and ecosystem risk

2. User-Based Valuation Models:

This approach is common in the tech sector and values the platform based on its user base and engagement quality:

Platform Value = Active Users × Customer Lifetime Value (CLV) × Engagement Index

3. Option-Based or Strategic Valuation:

Platforms are often innovation enablers with optionality value. Their worth lies in what they allow:

- Spinouts (e.g. training arms, marketplaces)
- Ecosystem leverage (e.g. data collaborations, APIs)

- Strategic positioning (e.g. regulatory influence, standards leadership)

Practical Use in Association Strategy

Boards and CFOs can use capital valuation frameworks to:

- Justify platform infrastructure investment
- Structure joint ventures or licensing partnerships
- Demonstrate the long-term value of intangible assets (e.g. trust, engagement, behavioural data)
- Evaluate potential exit strategies or commercialisation options

Boardroom Reflection Questions

- Are we building a service, or an asset?
- Have we valued our data, platform infrastructure, or ecosystem position?
- What strategic options does our platform enable?
- Could part of our platform become a spinout, partnership, or licensed offering?
- Are we stewarding this platform as a capital asset or a program cost?

Valuing the platform business model reframes digital transformation as capital formation. Associations that understand, measure, and govern their platform's capital value will be better positioned to make long-term, strategic investment decisions, and to secure the partnerships and funding needed to realise their potential.

Chapter 22. Financial and Pricing Maturity Models

Assessing the Readiness of Your Cost Structures and Monetisation Strategies

This annexure introduces two integrated five-level maturity models to evaluate how well an association's financial and pricing strategies align with a platform business model. It is designed for use by CFOs, finance committees, and boards seeking to:

- Benchmark their organisation's financial planning sophistication,
- Assess the strategic adequacy of current pricing structures, and
- Identify capability gaps that may constrain platform transformation.

These models do not prescribe a "one-size-fits-all" approach. Rather, they offer a diagnostic framework to inform investment in financial capability, pricing innovation, and governance oversight.

Why Maturity Matters in Platform Contexts

Traditional association models often rely on flat pricing and static forecasting. But platform models demand dynamic planning, behavioural segmentation, and scenario-ready financial tools.

Key shifts include:

Table 22-1 Maturity Matters

Traditional Model	Platform Model
Flat pricing tiers	Demand-based segmentation
Manual forecasts	Predictive, data-driven modelling
Fixed budgets	Flexible financial infrastructure
Static revenue mix	Diversified, multi-sided streams

Without upgrading financial and pricing maturity, platform strategies remain brittle, reactive, or misaligned.

Financial Model Maturity Framework

This five-level model evaluates how effectively an association plans, forecasts, and models financial performance.

Table 22-2 Financial Model Maturity

Level	Approach	Key Characteristics	Improvement Path
1. Inadequate	Ad-hoc projections	Intuition-driven; lacks structure or data	Start with historical baselines; capture fixed and variable costs
2. Basic	Static spreadsheets	Fixed assumptions, limited scenario testing	Introduce revenue metrics (e.g. CLV, CPA)
3. Intermediate	Dynamic spreadsheets	Multi-scenario, basic segmentation	Automate updates, integrate real-time data feeds
4. Advanced	Financial modelling software	Automated, benchmarkable models	Link to BI tools and CRM/AMS systems
5. Robust	Predictive, real-time models	AI/ML, scenario simulations, visual dashboards	Model churn, cohort growth, pricing elasticity

Board Question: Where does our financial planning sit on this spectrum, and does it support our strategic ambitions?

Pricing Model Maturity Framework

This model assesses the association's ability to price strategically in a multi-sided environment. Pricing is no longer just a finance decision, it is a value and engagement lever.

Table 22-3 Pricing Model Maturity

Level	Approach	Key Characteristics	Next-Step Opportunities
1. Inadequate	Flat pricing	Uniform pricing, low engagement	Begin with segmentation by need/value
2. Basic	Simple tiers	2–3 pricing levels, no elasticity data	Introduce Cu (cost per user) and WTP data
3. Intermediate	Dynamic tiering	Pricing reflects usage, preferences	Pilot A/B pricing tests; analyse outcomes
4. Advanced	Data-informed pricing	Elasticity curves, marginal cost modelling	Behaviour-driven tiers and micro-targeting

Level	Approach	Key Characteristics	Next-Step Opportunities
5. Predictive	AI-optimised pricing	Real-time adjustments based on demand	Full lifecycle pricing using ML insights

Board Question: Are we using pricing as a strategic tool, or relying on historical assumptions?

Linking Maturity to Monetisation Strategy

As financial and pricing maturity increase, associations unlock:

- Scenario planning capacity
- Flexible revenue experimentation
- Segment-specific pricing offers
- Better alignment of pricing with value perception

Higher maturity also supports equity and fairness in pricing decisions through data transparency, value segmentation and clear understanding of the membership value proposition.

Governance Use Cases

Boards and executives can use these maturity ladders to:

- **Assess capability gaps** before launching new pricing models or products
- **Benchmark** progress year-over-year
- **Support investment decisions** in digital finance tools or pricing intelligence
- **Guide oversight** of risk and fairness in revenue strategy

Boardroom Reflection Questions

- Are we pricing based on cost, demand, or value perception?
- Can our current financial tools model multi-sided revenue scenarios?
- How fast can we test, adjust, or sunset a pricing model?
- What governance oversight do we have over pricing fairness and strategic trade-offs?
- What capabilities would we need to reach the next level of maturity?

Conclusion

Platform success requires more than vision, it demands financial and pricing capabilities that can keep pace with strategic complexity and digital scale. These maturity models provide a clear, actionable roadmap for associations ready to move beyond spreadsheets and into scenario-driven, member-informed financial leadership.

Boards, CFOs, and executives should revisit these models annually as part of their strategy, budgeting, or digital transformation cycles.

Glossary

Adaptive Governance: A governance approach that enables rapid, insight-informed decision-making in complex and changing environments. Emphasises learning, agility, and cultural responsiveness. *See also: Agile Governance; Governance Capability*

Agile Governance: A model of governance that prioritises responsiveness, transparency, and ethical oversight. It replaces rigid oversight structures with dynamic mechanisms for real-time risk management and participatory input. *See also: Governance Maturity; Trust Infrastructure*

APPS Scorecard: The Association Platform Performance Scorecard is a diagnostic tool for assessing an association's platform maturity across core domains: infrastructure, insight, governance, and engagement. *See also: Platform Readiness; Diagnostic Tools*

Association Platform Success Framework (APSF): A foundational model introduced in Chapter 2 that integrates five design pillars: scalable infrastructure, data insight, modular experience, participation strategy, and governance/trust. *See also: Platform Thinking; Enabling Layers*

Behavioural Governance: Focuses on how decisions are made, examining trust, board dynamics, values, and leadership culture. One of the three governance capability domains. *See also: Governance Capability; Culture Maturity*

Boardroom Capability: Refers to the skills, digital fluency, and adaptive leadership required at board level to govern complex, platform-based associations. *See also: Capability Domain; Governance Maturity*

Business Model Innovation: The process of reimagining how value is created, delivered, and captured. In platform-based associations, this includes transitioning to multi-sided models and non-linear revenue flows. *See also: Monetisation Models; Platform Economics*

Capability Domain: One of the three governance capability domains. Focuses on the skills, confidence, and digital readiness of the board and executive team. *See also: Structure Domain; Behavioural Governance*

Co-Design: A participatory design method where members, users, and stakeholders collaborate in developing services, policies, or platforms. *See also: Participation Strategy; Member Experience Lab*

Crowd Contribution: Value generated through user input, peer learning, co-creation, or member-generated content. A key feature of scalable platform engagement. *See also: Marketplace Model; Network Effects*

Data-Driven Insight: The use of analytics, segmentation, and predictive modelling to inform strategy and improve member experiences. One of the APSF pillars. *See also: Insight Maturity; Strategic Data Capability*

Diagnostic Continuum: The tool for assessing Governance Friction, from Harmony through Friction to Conflict and Collapse. Supports early intervention and realignment. *See also: Governance Friction; Adaptive Governance*

Digital Risk Threshold: A governance mechanism that defines acceptable risk boundaries for digital tools, AI systems, and data practices. *See also: Ethical AI; Scenario Testing*

Dynamic Risk Intelligence: A real-time, adaptive capability that enables organisations to sense, interpret, and respond to emerging risks across complex systems and digital environments. It integrates predictive analytics, scenario modelling, and human judgment to anticipate friction points, detect weak signals, and enable timely governance interventions. Supports decision-making under uncertainty by fusing structured data with contextual insight. *See also: Diagnostic Continuum; Scenario Testing; Adaptive Governance*

Ecosystem

A dynamic network of interconnected organisations, individuals, platforms, and resources that collaboratively create and exchange value. In the context of associations, ecosystems extend beyond traditional member-service models to include partners, platforms, funders, beneficiaries, and data contributors, often operating under shared governance or aligned purpose. Well-designed ecosystems enable adaptability, co-creation, and scale by leveraging network effects and shared infrastructure. See also: *Ecosystem Leverage; Platform Orchestration; Participation Strategy*

Ecosystem Leverage: Using partnerships, networks, and third-party contributors to scale impact and value creation. Central to the platform mindset. *See also: Platform Orchestration; Multi-Sided Models*

Enabling Layers: Refers to the infrastructure, governance frameworks, and technical capabilities that allow platform associations to scale responsibly. *See also: Enabling Capabilities; Strategic Infrastructure*

Ethical AI: The design and governance of artificial intelligence systems that align with ethical standards, transparency, and human oversight. *See also: ISO 42001; Trust Infrastructure*

Foresight Capability: A board's ability to anticipate emerging risks, opportunities, and signals through scenario planning and horizon scanning. *See also: Future Readiness; Strategic Risk Intelligence*

Freemium Model: A monetisation strategy that offers free baseline access with optional paid upgrades. Common in content, CPD, and community platforms. *See also: Monetisation Pathways; Subscription Models*

Future Readiness Radar: A visual diagnostic tool for assessing preparedness across digital, economic, and governance dimensions. *See also: APPS Scorecard; Scenario Testing*

Governance Capability: A multi-dimensional measure of a board's ability to govern effectively. Includes structure, behaviour, and capability. *See also: ISO 37004; Governance Maturity*

Governance Friction: The tension or misalignment that emerges when governance structures are no longer fit-for-purpose in changing environments. *See also: Diagnostic Continuum; Friction-to-Function Model*

Governance Maturity: The evolution of governance systems from compliance-based to strategic and adaptive. Often measured using tools like the Maturity Matrix. *See also: Agile Governance; Capability Domains*

Insight Maturity: Describes an association's capacity to turn raw data into decision-ready insight. A key enabler of strategic agility. *See also: Strategic Data Capability; Dashboards*

ISO 37000 Series: A suite of international standards on governance, including ISO 37000 (principles), ISO 37004 (maturity models), and ISO 37005 (governance indicators). *See also: Capability Domains; Governance Assessment*

Marketplace Model: A business model in which the association acts as a platform enabling transactions between users (e.g. CPD courses, services, mentoring). *See also: Multi-Sided Revenue; Platform Ecosystem*

Member Experience Lab: A method for involving members in the co-design and testing of new services and engagement strategies. *See also: Co-Design; Participation Architecture*

Modular Design: Designing content, services, and systems in flexible, customisable units that can be recombined or scaled across use cases. *See also: Product Strategy; Freemium Models*

Monetisation Pathways: The range of strategies available for generating revenue, direct and indirect, member- and partner-based. *See also: Platform Revenue Model Matrix; Business Model Innovation*

Multi-Sided Revenue: Income derived from multiple sources beyond members, such as sponsors, advertisers, partners, and data clients. *See also: Network Effects; Platform Economics*

Network Effects: The phenomenon where the value of a platform increases as more users participate. Includes both direct and indirect effects. *See also: Platform Economics; Ecosystem Leverage*

Participation Strategy: A deliberate approach to designing how members and stakeholders engage, contribute, and create value within the platform. *See also: Ecosystem Participation; Value Co-Creation*

Platform Economics: An economic model where value is co-created by users, marginal costs decline with scale, and growth is driven by network effects. *See also: Multi-Sided Revenue; Value Multiplication*

Platform Orchestration: The strategic role of an association in enabling and managing multi-party interactions within an ecosystem. *See also: Ecosystem Leverage; Governance and Trust*

Platform Posture: An association's overall orientation to platform strategy, including how it designs for value exchange, openness, and strategic growth. *See also: APSF; Business Model Transformation*

Risk Appetite: The amount and type of risk an organisation is willing to accept in pursuit of its goals. It guides decision-making and sets boundaries for strategic and operational risk-taking. See also: *Governance Capability; Risk Management Framework*

Risk Management Framework: A structured approach to identifying, assessing, mitigating, and monitoring risks across an organisation. It ensures risk is managed consistently and transparently in line with strategic objectives.: See also: *Governance Maturity; Scenario Testing*

Scenario Testing: A practice used by boards to explore future risks and decisions through hypothetical but plausible situations. *See also: Risk Intelligence; Simulation Tools*

Trust Infrastructure: The frameworks, policies, and behaviours that ensure ethical oversight, data integrity, and reciprocal value exchange. *See also: Governance and Trust; Ethical AI*

Detailed Table of Contents

Tables of Tables

Bibliography

Aagaard, A. & Tucci, C. (2024). AI-Driven Business Model Innovation: Pioneering New Frontiers in Value Creation. In A. Aagaard (Ed.), Business Model Innovation: Game Changers and Contemporary Issues (pp. 295–329). Palgrave Macmillan. https://doi.org/10.1007/978-3-031-57511-2_10

Aagaard, A. (2024). Business model innovation: Game changers and contemporary issues. Palgrave Macmillan.

Aagaard, A. (2024). Introducing Business Model Innovation and the Game Changers of Tomorrow. In A. Aagaard (Ed.), Business Model Innovation: Game Changers and Contemporary Issues (pp. 1–26). Palgrave Macmillan. https://doi.org/10.1007/978-3-031-57511-2_1

Adner, R. (2017). Ecosystem as structure: An actionable construct for strategy. Journal of Management, 43(1), 39–58. https://doi.org/10.1177/0149206316678451

Agrawal, A. Gans, J. & Goldfarb, A. (2018). Prediction Machines: The Simple Economics of Artificial Intelligence. Harvard Business Review Press.

AHRI (Australian HR Institute). (2023). Annual Transparency Report. www.ahri.com.au

AHRI Annual Report 2022; AHRI Capability Framework.

Allen, D. W. E. Berg, C. & Davidson, S. (2023). The Exchange Theory of Web3 Governance.

Allen, D. W. E. Berg, C. Davidson, S. Gettler, L. Kane, E. Lane, A. M. & Potts, J. (2020). So, You Run a University?

AMI (Australian Marketing Institute). (2023). Flexible Membership Models for a Changing Market. Retrieved from https://ami.org.au/membership

Austin, J. E. & Seitanidi, M. M. (2012). Collaborative Value Creation: A Review of Partnering Between Nonprofits and Businesses. Nonprofit and Voluntary Sector Quarterly, 42(5), 739–768. https://doi.org/10.1177/0899764012454685

Australian Institute of Company Directors (AICD). (2023). Governing through uncertainty: Lessons for boards on transformation and risk. https://aicd.companydirectors.com.au

Brynjolfsson, E. & McAfee, A. (2017). Machine, Platform, Crowd: Harnessing Our Digital Future. W. W. Norton & Company.

Bryson, J. M. (2018). Strategic planning for public and nonprofit organizations: A guide to strengthening and sustaining organizational achievement (5th ed.). Jossey-Bass.

Budden, P. & Murray, F. (2022). Strategically engaging with innovation ecosystems. MIT Sloan Management Review, 64(1), 38-43. https://mitsloan.mit.edu/

Budden, P. & Murray, F. (2025). Accelerating Innovation: Competitive Advantage through Ecosystem Engagement. MIT Press.

Chait, R. P. Ryan, W. P. & Taylor, B. E. (2005). Governance as Leadership: Reframing the Work of Nonprofit Boards. Wiley.

Chesbrough, H. (2006). Open Innovation: The New Imperative for Creating and Profiting from Technology. Harvard Business Review Press.

Coase, R. H. (1937). The Nature of the Firm. Economica, 4(16), 386-405.

Cornforth, C. (2003). The Governance of Public and Non-Profit Organizations: What Do Boards Do? Routledge.

Cusumano, M. A. Gawer, A. & Yoffie, D. B. (2019). The Business of Platforms: Strategy in the Age of Digital Competition, Innovation, and Power. Harper Business.

Davidson, S. De Filippi, P. & Potts, J. (2018). Blockchains and the economic institutions of capitalism. Journal of Institutional Economics, 14(4), 639–658. https://doi.org/10.1017/S1744137417000200

Davidson, S. Novak, M. & Potts, J. (2018). The Cost of Trust: A Pilot Study on Blockchain Governance. Journal of Institutional Economics, 14(6), 1065-1087.

De Filippi, P. & Wright, A. (2018). Blockchain and the Law: The Rule of Code. Harvard University Press.

Deloitte Global Risk Advisory. (2022). The connecting force: Risk intelligence platforms enabling decisions (Issue 2). Deloitte. Retrieved from https://www.deloitte.com

Deloitte. (2020). The Boardroom Frontier: Redefining Governance in the Digital Age. Retrieved from www.deloitte.com

Deloitte. (2023). CEO Survey: Ecosystems and platforms for growth. Deloitte Insights. https://www2.deloitte.com/

Drucker, P. F. (1990). Managing the nonprofit organization: Principles and practices. HarperBusiness.

Elkington, J. (1997). Cannibals with Forks: The Triple Bottom Line of 21st Century Business. Capstone Publishing.

Eric von Hippel. (2005). Democratizing innovation. MIT Press.

European Commission. (2021). Proposal for a Regulation Laying Down Harmonised Rules on Artificial Intelligence (AI Act).

Evans, D. S. & Schmalensee, R. (2008). Catalyst Code: The Strategies Behind the World's Most Dynamic Companies. Harvard Business Review Press.

Evans, D. S. & Schmalensee, R. (2011). Platform Economics: Essays on Multi-Sided Businesses. Competition Policy International.

Evans, D. S. & Schmalensee, R. (2016). Matchmakers: The New Economics of Multisided Platforms. Harvard Business Review Press.

Evans, D. S. Schmalensee, R. Noel, M. D. Chang, H. H. & Garcia-Swartz, D. D. (2011). Platform Economics: Essays on Multi-Sided Businesses. Competition Policy International.

Evans, P. C. & Gawer, A. (2016). The Rise of the Platform Enterprise: A Global Survey. Center for Global Enterprise.

Fenwick, M. & Vermeulen, E. P. (2018). Technology and Corporate Governance: Blockchain, Crypto, and Artificial Intelligence. SSRN Electronic Journal. https://doi.org/10.2139/ssrn.3285524.

Freeman, R. E. (1984). Strategic management: A stakeholder approach. Pitman Publishing.

Frumkin, P. (2002). On being nonprofit: A conceptual and policy primer. Harvard University Press.

Gawer, A. & Cusumano, M. A. (2014). Industry Platforms and Ecosystem Innovation. Journal of Product Innovation Management, 31(3), 417–433.

Gawer, A. Cusumano, M. A. & Yoffie, D. B. (2023). The Platform Organization. In C. Snow & Ø. Fjeldstad (Eds.), Designing Modern Organizations. Cambridge University Press.

Gawer, A. (2020). Digital Platforms' Boundaries: The Interplay of Firm Scope, Platform Sides, and Digital Interfaces. Long Range Planning, 54(5), 102045. https://doi.org/10.1016/j.lrp.2020.102045

Governance Institute of Australia. (2024). Micro-credentials and digital badges. Retrieved April 20, 2025, from https://www.governanceinstitute.com.au/education/micro-credentials/

Hagiu, A. & Wright, J. (2015). Marketplace or Reseller?. Management Science, 61(1), 184–203.

Hansmann, H. (1980). The role of nonprofit enterprise. The Yale Law Journal, 89(5), 835–901. https://doi.org/10.2307/796089

Heifetz, R. Grashow, A. & Linsky, M. (2009). The practice of adaptive leadership: Tools and tactics for changing your organization and the world. Harvard Business Press.
Hein, A. Schreieck, M. Wiesche, M. & Krcmar, H. (2016). Multiple-Case Analysis on Governance Mechanisms of Multi-Sided Platforms. Journal of Information Technology, 31(2), 1–10.
Herman, R. D. & Renz, D. O. (2008). Advancing nonprofit organizational effectiveness research and theory: Nine theses. Nonprofit Management and Leadership, 18(4), 399–415. https://doi.org/10.1002/nml.195
Iansiti, M. & Levien, R. (2004). The Keystone Advantage: What the New Dynamics of Business Ecosystems Mean for Strategy, Innovation, and Sustainability. Harvard Business Review Press.
International Organization for Standardization (ISO). (2021). ISO/IEC 27001:2021: Information Security, Cybersecurity and Privacy Protection: Information Security Management Systems. Geneva: ISO.
International Organization for Standardization (ISO). (2023). ISO 37000:2023: Governance of Organizations. Geneva: ISO.
International Organization for Standardization (ISO). (2023). ISO/IEC 42001:2023 - Artificial Intelligence - Management System. Geneva, Switzerland: ISO.
International Organization for Standardization (ISO)(2018). ISO 31000:2018 Risk Management: Guidelines. International Organization for Standardization.
International Organization for Standardization (ISO) (2021). ISO 37000:2021 Governance of organizations: Guidance. International Organization for Standardization. https://www.iso.org/standard/65036.html
IRM (2024). Setting the Risk Agenda: Exploring the Future of the Risk Management Profession. Institute of Risk Management.
Jacobides, M. G. Cennamo, C. & Gawer, A. (2018). Towards a Theory of Ecosystems. Strategic Management Journal, 39(8), 2255–2276. https://doi.org/10.1002/smj.2904
Jacobs, C. & Goddard, M. (2020). Adaptive Governance: The Next Frontier for Board Effectiveness. Journal of Governance & Accountability Studies, 14(2), 215-238.
Jobin, A. Ienca, M. & Vayena, E. (2019). The Global Landscape of AI Ethics Guidelines. Nature Machine Intelligence, 1(9), 389-399.
Kania, J. & Kramer, M. (2011). Collective Impact. Stanford Social Innovation Review, 9(1), 36–41.
Kaplan, R. S. & Norton, D. P. (1996). The Balanced Scorecard: Translating Strategy into Action. Harvard Business Review Press.
Kegan, R. & Lahey, L. L. (2009). Immunity to change: How to overcome it and unlock the potential in yourself and your organization. Harvard Business Press.
Lewin, K. (1947). Frontiers in Group Dynamics: Concept, Method and Reality in Social Science; Social Equilibria and Social Change. Human Relations, 1(1), 5-41V 2.7
Markova, G. Ford, R. C. Dickson, D. R. & Bohn, T. M. (2013). Professional associations and members' benefits: What's in it for me? Nonprofit Management and Leadership, 23(4), 491–510. https://doi.org/10.1002/nml.21075
Marty, F. & Warin, T. (2023). Multi-Sided Platforms and Innovation. Harvard Business Review.
Mayer, R. C. Davis, J. H. & Schoorman, F. D. (1995). An integrative model of organizational trust. Academy of Management Review, 20(3), 709–734.
McCrindle Research. (2023). The future of education, employment and engagement in Australia. https://mccrindle.com.au/
MCI Group. (2024). Global association benchmarking report. https://www.mci-group.com/
McKinley Advisors. (2022). Association viewpoint: An age of acceleration. McKinley Advisors. https://www.mckinley-advisors.com

McKinsey & Company. (2024). Rewired: The Future of Digital Transformation. McKinsey Digital.

Miehé, L. & Gassmann, O. (2024). New Venues for Collaborative Business Model Innovation Through Ecosystems. In A. Aagaard (Ed.), Business Model Innovation: Game Changers and Contemporary Issues (pp. 57–87). Palgrave Macmillan. https://doi.org/10.1007/978-3-031-57511-2_3

Mintzberg, H. Ahlstrand, B. W. & Lampel, J. (1998). Strategy safari: A guided tour through the wilds of strategic management. Free Press.

NIST. (2018). Framework for Improving Critical Infrastructure Cybersecurity (Version 1.1). National Institute of Standards and Technology.

OECD. (2021). Collaborative innovation: Transforming public sector ecosystems. https://www.oecd.org/

OECD. (2023). Good governance for critical infrastructure resilience. OECD Publishing. https://doi.org/10.1787/3f4a2f31-en

Osterwalder, A. & Pigneur, Y. (2010). Business Model Generation: A Handbook for Visionaries, Game Changers, and Challengers. Wiley.

Parker, G. Van Alstyne, M. & Choudary, S. (2016). Platform Revolution: How Networked Markets are Transforming the Economy. W. W. Norton & Company.

Porter, M. E. (2011). Creating Shared Value. Harvard Business Review, 89(1/2), 62–77.

Potts, J. (2025). von Hippel innovation. Prometheus, 40(2), 74-91.

Potts, J. (2025). Von Hippel Innovation: Innovation as Infrastructure. In Wennberg, K. & Sandström, C. (Eds.), Questioning the Entrepreneurial State. Springer.

Professional Advantage. (2023, September 21). Governance Institute of Australia: Going all-in on cloud to focus on members. Retrieved April 20, 2025, from https://www.pa.com.au/client-success/governance-institute-of-australia/

Putnam, R. D. (2000). Bowling Alone: The Collapse and Revival of American Community. Simon & Schuster.

Ray, P. P. (2023). Web3: A Comprehensive Review on Background, Technologies, Applications, Zero-Trust Architectures, Challenges, and Future Directions. Internet of Things and Cyber-Physical Systems, 3, 213–248.

Reim, W. Sjödin, D. & Parida, V. (2023). Enabling Collaboration on Digital Platforms: A Study of Digital Twins. Journal of Business Research.

Ritala, P. & Jovanovic, M. (2024). Platformizers, Orchestrators, and Guardians: B2B Models for Digital Ecosystems. Working Paper.

Ritala, P. & Jovanovic, M. (2024). Platformizers, Orchestrators, and Guardians: Strategies for Managing Multi-Sided Platform Ecosystems.

Ritala, P. & Jovanovic, M. (2024). Platformizers, orchestrators, and guardians: Three archetypes for digital platform business models. California Management Review, 66(2), 78–96.

Ritala, P. & Jovanovic, M. (2024). Platformizers, Orchestrators, and Guardians: Three Types of B2B Platform Business Models. In A. Aagaard & C. Nielsen (Eds.), Business Model Innovation: Game Changers and Contemporary Issues (pp. 75–91). Palgrave Macmillan.

Rochet, J. C. & Tirole, J. (2003). Platform Competition in Two-Sided Markets. Journal of the European Economic Association, 1(4), 990–1029.

Rochet, J.C. & Tirole, J. (2006). Two-sided markets: A progress report. RAND Journal of Economics, 37(3), 645–667.

Rumelt, Richard. (2022). The crux: How leaders become strategists. Profile Books.

Saadatmanesh, H. (2022). AI-enabled: Transforming Digital Business Models. Technological Forecasting and Social Change, 183, 121912.

Saadatmanesh, H. (2022). AI-Enabled Dynamic Capabilities for Transforming Digital Business Models to Smart Business Models. University of Oulu

Sankur, A. et al. (2024). True Customer-Centricity: An Operating Model for Competitive Advantage. McKinsey & Company.

Sattlegger, A. & Bharosa, N. (2024). Beyond principles: Embedding ethical AI risks in public sector risk management practice. Proceedings of the 25th Annual International Conference on Digital Government Research (DGO 2024), Taipei, Taiwan, June 11–14, 2024. ACM. https://doi.org/10.1145/3657054.3657063

Schrepel, T. (2019). Collusion by Blockchain and Smart Contracts. Harvard Journal of Law & Technology, 33(2), 1–44. https://doi.org/10.2139/ssrn.3242860.

Schumpeter, J. A. (1942). Capitalism, Socialism, and Democracy. Harper & Brothers.

Senge, P. M. (1990). The fifth discipline: The art and practice of the learning organization. Doubleday.

Srnicek, N. (2017). Platform Capitalism. Polity Press.

Staykova, K. S. & Damsgaard, J. (2015). A Typology of Multi-Sided Platforms: The Core and the Periphery. European Conference on Information Systems (ECIS).

Susskind, R. & Susskind, D. (2015). The future of the professions: How technology will transform the work of human experts. Oxford University Press.

Szabo, N. (1997). Formalizing and Securing Relationships on Public Networks. First Monday, 2(9).

Teece, D. J. (2010). Business Models, Business Strategy and Innovation. Long Range Planning, 43(2–3), 172–194.https://doi.org/10.1016/j.lrp.2009.07.003

Tejero, A. Márquez, J. A. & Dodero, J. M. (2020). University as a Platform: An Evolutionary Process Towards an Open Educational Ecosystem in Europe. Open Science Framework

Tiwana, A. (2014). Platform Ecosystems: Aligning Architecture, Governance, and Strategy. Morgan Kaufmann.

Tucci, C. L. Afuah, A. & Viscusi, G. (2018). Creating and capturing value through digital platforms. MIT Sloan Management Review, 60(1), 21–27.

Tuckman, H. P. & Chang, C. F. (1991). A Methodology for Measuring the Financial Vulnerability of Charitable Nonprofit Organizations. Nonprofit and Voluntary Sector Quarterly, 20(4), 445-460.

von Hippel, E. (2005). Democratizing Innovation. MIT Press.

Weisbrod, B. A. (1988). The nonprofit economy. Harvard University Press.

West, M. A. (2021). Compassionate leadership: Sustaining wisdom, humanity and presence in health and social care. Swirling Leaf Press.

Williamson, B. (2019). Policy Networks, Performance Metrics, and Platform Markets. Journal of Economic Policy Research.

Williamson, O. E. (1975). Markets and Hierarchies: Analysis and Antitrust Implications. Free Press

Williamson, O. E. (1981). The Economics of Organization: The Transaction Cost Approach. American Journal of Sociology, 87(3), 548-577.

World Economic Forum. (2020). The board's guide to artificial intelligence. https://www.weforum.org/whitepapers/the-board-s-guide-to-artificial-intelligence

World Economic Forum. (2024). Future of Jobs Report 2024. https://www.weforum.org/reports/future-of-jobs-report-2024

Yablonsky, S. A. (2019). Multi-Sided Platforms: Current State and Future Research. Russian Management Journal, 17(4), 519–546.

Young, D. R. (2007). Financing nonprofits: Putting theory into practice. Rowman & Littlefield.

Lakefield Drive Publishing

Sean M Johnson FGIA MAICD LLB MBA GCertEd

Lakefield Drive Pty Ltd
Australia
info@lakefielddrive.co
https://lakefielddrive.co/

lakefield
drive

Other Books

The Modern Association Playbook: Reimagining Strategy, Governance, and Value Creation

What if your association could lead transformation and not just respond to it?

In a time of digital disruption, declining member trust, and growing complexity, traditional association models are under strain. Incremental change is no longer enough. Strategic evolution is now essential and is required across purpose, business model, and governance.

The Modern Association Playbook equips boards, executives, and association professionals with the tools and frameworks to build future-ready organisations. Grounded in real-world advisory experience and written for practical boardroom use, it combines platform thinking, economic insight, and agile governance into a roadmap for relevance and renewal.

Inside, you'll learn how to:

- Reframe member value through ecosystem design
- Pivot your association business model with confidence
- Embed agility and ethics into governance and technology
- Drive engagement, resilience, and long-term impact

Whether you lead a national peak body, professional society, or grassroots organisation, this playbook offers a strategic blueprint to modernise with purpose, clarity, and credibility.

Smart. Practical. Board-ready. This is your guide to modern association leadership, designed for those ready to shape the future, not just survive it.

The Modern Association Playbook | Lakefield Drive

https://lakefielddrive.co/the-modern-association-pb

https://www.amazon.com.au/Modern-Association-Playbook-Reimagining-Governance/dp/1764072707/

Made in United States
North Haven, CT
04 November 2026

21760290R00137